Explorations in the

ORDINARY

Credits

Some of the essays included in this volume originally appeared in magazines. Most have been substantially revised for book publication. Grateful acknowledgement is extended to the editors of these publications.

A portion of the Introduction appeared in *Minnesota Calls*, June 1990 (Vol. 3, No. 5).

"One Small Sight, One Soft Sound," *Minnesota Calls*, July 1990 (Vol. 3, No. 6).

"A Falling Star," *Minnesota Calls*, August 1990 (Vol. 3, No. 7). Also in *Country*, 1992.

"The White-Fronted Goose," *Minnesota Calls*, Sept./Oct. 1990 (Vol. 3, No. 8).

"Ghosts of Autumn," *Minnesota Calls*, Nov./Dec. 1990 (Vol. 3, No. 9).

"In the Heart of the Waterfall," *Minnesota Calls*, Jan./Feb. 1991 (Vol. 4, No. 1).

"A Sprouting of Spring," *Minnesota Calls*, March/April 1991 (Vol. 4, No. 2).

"An Encounter with Innocence," *Minnesota Calls*, May/June 1991 (Vol. 4, No. 3).

"Rain, Sand, and Shattered Wings," *Minnesota Calls*, July/Aug. 1991 (Vol. 4, No. 4).

"One Tiny Fall," *Minnesota Calls*, Sept./Oct. 1991 (Vol. 4, No. 5).

"Bittersweet Thoughts," *Minnesota Calls*, Nov./Dec. 1991 (Vol. 4, No. 6).

"On the Track," *Minnesota Calls*, Jan./Feb. 1992 (Vol. 5, No. 1).

"Bones of the Forest," *Minnesota Calls*, March/April 1992 (Vol. 5, No. 2).

"Under the Umbrella," *Minnesota Calls*, May/June 1992 (Vol. 5, No. 3).

Explorations
in the
Ordinary

A Backyard Naturalist's
View of Minnesota

ഔ ൠ

David R. Moffatt

NORTH STAR PRESS OF ST. CLOUD, INC.

For Joan,
Who brought me Spring.

Cover photo by David R. Moffatt

Unless otherwise indicated, all photos by David R. Moffatt

Library of Congress Cataloging-in-Publication Data
Moffatt, David R., 1963-
    Explorations in the ordinary : a backyard naturalist's
view of Minnesota / David R. Moffatt.
    128 p. 23 cm.
    ISBN 0-87839-099-5
    1. Nature. I. Title.
QH81.M737 1996
508--dc20   96-23889
                                                        CIP

Printed in the United States of America by Versa Press, Inc., of
East Peoria, Illinois.

Published by: North Star Press of St. Cloud, Inc.
                     P.O. Box 451
                     St. Cloud, Minnesota 56302

Contents

Introduction

"I have traveled extensively in Concord," wrote Henry David Thoreau. Thoreau, a wise man, knew that the true value of travel lies not in the number of miles but the quantity of ideas, impressions, and observations involved.

In my work as a writer and nature photographer, I have been privileged to observe any number of unusual natural phenomena and to visit some thoroughly out-of-the-way sites. It has, however, been my experience that the most intriguing aspects of nature are often those that are most ordinary on first glance.

The following essays were composed over a period of several years and were inspired by a variety of events, moods, and seasons. Each is an attempt to explore, in one way or another, my belief that the most profound lessons in the natural world lie more often among the small than the great, with the ordinary more often than the rare. A dandelion viewed through receptive eyes possesses a complexity and beauty equal to that of the most exotic orchid, and an agate plucked from the shore of a lake holds within its myriad veins and shades a wonder that eyes attracted only to diamonds will never know.

I will offer little discussion of familiar landmarks in the pages that follow—indeed, I embrace a certain ambiguity about the locations visited. My hope is to explore the landmarks, real and metaphorical, found in any natural locale and to instill in the reader some desire to do the same. While each of the places and events described in this volume is very real, I hope to lead readers' eyes to their own monuments, rather than tempt anyone to search for mine.

A hilltop seems as appropriate a place as any to begin, an ordinary hilltop on which, several years ago, I happened upon a rather extraordinary find—a dead basswood tree, recently deceased if the drying leaves clinging to a few branches were any indication. A narrow strip of leathery-grey bark had been peeled from the trunk in an almost perfect spiral that began high above my head and ended at ground level.

The bone-white band of exposed wood wound so symmetrically around the tree that one might have suspected mischievous hands at work with carefully guided tools. Which was, in a sense, the case. But the hands involved were those of nature, and the tool employed was a powerful arc of static electricity—a bolt of lightning. Had I cared to dig beneath the dead roots, I might have found a fulgurite—a fused, glassy mass of soil formed by the passing of the fatal stroke into the earth.

Aside from the curious markings left upon the trunk by the forces that had destroyed it, the basswood's appearance displayed nothing to suggest uniqueness. I wondered why it, of the hundreds of trees in the surrounding area, had attracted lightning.

Self-proclaimed authorities disagree as to whether certain species of trees "draw" lightning—scientists say no, devotees of folk wisdom insist otherwise, usually claiming that the water content of a tree trunk affects its chances of being electrocuted. The basswood is a veritable water barrel, as anyone who has cut into a living one can testify. Perhaps it was that which drew the bolt of lightning into the tree to flash its sap into steam and blow shreds of bark in every direction (a search turned up pieces of basswood bark more than one hundred feet away).

The oak, however, is the tree with the highest water content. Yet, three white oaks stood quite near the basswood, all of them in perfect health.

I thought, too, of the hilltop location, of the old axiom about lightning always striking the highest point in a given area. But the basswood was shorter than several of its immediate neighbors, topping out at least ten feet below the height of trees only a few feet away.

Folklore is rife with stories, probably untrue, of images of human faces being etched into windows by the flash from a lightning bolt. Lightning has been known to kill people outright, while merely knocking others out of their shoes. Whether one is guided by folklore, statistics, or the science of natural history, it is difficult to avoid the conclusion that lightning is guided by nothing so much as a curious brand of whimsy.

I do not know why the hilltop basswood proved to have a fatal attraction for lightning. In the web of life that is the natural world, the countless events and conditions that lead to any occurrence may be impossible to unravel sufficiently for the human mind to sort. Much, too, may appear random to our eyes but is carefully governed by rules we have not yet learned to read. World weather patterns, some now say, are altered infinitesimally by every flap of a butterfly's wing, and the earth's rotation is slowed ever so slightly by every splash of a wave upon a shore.

For whatever reason, an otherwise unremarkable basswood died a sudden death during a thunderstorm on an early summer day. These words commemorate it, but it stands as its own monument.

ℰ෨   ℭ෮

Of Iron, Woods, and Wonder

During a recent forest walk, I encountered a mystery. A small mystery, to be sure, but one forming the basis for speculations that may, in their own way, have some significance on a somewhat grander scale.

Winter's frost had been playing hide-and-seek, retreating from the topsoil by afternoon, only to return by morning. The mat of fallen leaves and last year's dead grass covering the forest earth lay sodden, dusted in places with cobwebby masses of snow mold, nearly silent underfoot. A hush held the forest. No birdsong, no scrabbling beneath the trees. Fallen seeds had long since been eaten; insects had not yet emerged from the soil. Winter's finches, chickadees, and nuthatches sat silent or had moved on. The first robin had not yet arrived. Wandering through a forested area not far from my home, I often found myself feeling uncomfortably alone.

Little color lightened the woods that day; the sky hid above featureless overcast, and what few shades persisted in winter's wake were so subtle and monotonous that my eyes quickly tired into ignoring them. Early spring is not a season of color, and eyes long dazzled by winter sunlight are not inclined to notice the somber shades it offers.

If bright color cannot be found in early spring, neither can straight lines be found in the forest. When I noticed an unnaturally straight vertical line during my walk, I altered my course to see what it could be. That it was man-made, I knew at once. Nature shapes constantly but has never been known to manufacture.

The object proved to be a stout iron rod, perhaps an inch in diameter and protruding about three feet from the ground. It had been driven into the earth so deeply that all my strength could not release it from the soil, still frozen below several inches of clinging mud. If the undisturbed rust coating the iron indicated age, the rod had kept its silent vigil for some time.

I thought little of the rod at first and walked on, considering it no more than a curiosity. Not for some time did I begin to wonder at the strangeness of encountering such an artifact half a mile from the nearest road, in a forest that only occasionally knew human presence.

Later I began to wonder about possible reasons for placing the iron rod in such an out-of-the-way spot. Perhaps it was something simple, a fence post or a marker of some sort. But no fences divided the woods in that area, and what anyone would find worthy of marking in such a remote place was quite beyond me.

I thought back to the history of the area, seeking an answer there. Logging swept throughout this part of the country. The trackless forest through which I walked, now filled with sprawling red oaks, gleaming birch, and the husks of dead elms, had been a solid expanse of proud Norway pines until the lumber companies left it as a sea of pitiful stumps over a century ago. Perhaps some long-ago lumberjack, for whatever reason, drove the rod into the ground and left it for the ages.

There was mining here, too, a series of turn-of-the-century efforts to find copper that ended in bankruptcy and allegations of fraud. The diligent searcher can still uncover traces of the old mines in several parts of the county, and the companies involved owned uncounted square miles of land at one time. Perhaps the rod was left behind during the course of a prospector's search. But what purpose it may have served, I have no idea.

The land on which I found the rod has passed through many hands in the past century. It has been logged, blasted, and tunneled; part of it was cleared and farmed for a while. Some distance from the rod, pieces of concrete and an overgrown roadbed show where a bridge once crossed a small stream. Human beings work their way with the land; the land regains itself but only with time. Traces of intrusion generally remain to puzzle the future.

In all likelihood, I will never know the true origin of the

rod I discovered sticking out of the ground in a remote forest area on a wet April afternoon. On a later visit to the area, I tried without success to relocate it. It remains out there, Sphinxlike with its silent question, for the next person to stumble upon the ordinary remnant of what may be an extraordinary tale.

ༀ   ༀ

The Bones of the Forest

The river passing through the lake near my home has been cutting through the rotting ice in recent days; yesterday it succeeded in clearing a path of open water all the way across. Within a week, the lake will shake itself completely free of the shell that has hidden it since mid-November. A strong wind may pile slabs of unwanted ice on the shore; more likely the ice will simply be absorbed by the water. The intense, clear blue of the open water always startles eyes numbed by the muted hues of winter.

I've been spending quite some time in the annual ritual of searching for green. No positive results yet, but, with the warming weather, it won't be much longer. Several grassy areas seem just a bit more alive now than several days ago, but perhaps wishful thinking makes them appear so.

However, signs of life hide in the forest. Dogwood branches blaze brilliant red, and here and there one encounters the white-fuzzed catkins of pussy willows peeping out like shy creatures undecided as to whether the proper time has come for them to emerge. The buds of some trees have begun to swell, particularly certain maples, whose tiny flowers will be the first blossoms of spring.

On a recent walk in search of new life, I passed through a stand of aspens. They looked as dead as they had appeared all winter; even up close, I could hardly tell that they were only sleeping now. When they awaken and leaf out, the process is fast, a week or so of rapid greening, after which I will hardly believe they had rested so long.

The aspen is one of the more immediately recognizable north woods trees. The slight greenish cast of its tightly bound bark sets it apart from the somewhat similar, but paler and

4

often peeling birch. Both trees share an abundant crown of shimmering leaves that dance and whisper with the slightest air movement.

Someone of moody temperament might notice the resemblance of a dormant stand of aspens to a procession of skeletons halted en route to some unknown destination. The bare, reaching limbs tipped with fingerlike twigs swaying in any breeze, the bleached trunks that seem to sway even when still, the whispers rising from the grove even when it is bare of leaves—there is something distinctly Halloweenish about it all. But the resemblance to a skeleton, to the framework of bone upon which all higher forms of life are constructed, runs deeper than mere appearance in the case of the aspen.

After a forest has been disturbed, by logging or burning or any of the ways in which trees are destroyed by humans or nature, some decades pass before the damage is erased. In my forest wanderings, I have more than once discovered the remains of stumps left by a fire that ravaged the nearby countryside in 1918.

Whether a forest is left a sea of stumps by loggers or a field of blackened earth by fire, the healing process begins

quickly. Grasses and wildflowers reappear right away, of course, but not far behind come flora of a more persistent variety.

Raspberries, blackberries, and prickly ash are generally the first woody plants to rise above a burned or cleared forest floor. Their fruit attracts birds, which, through their droppings, scatter seeds throughout the deforested area. Often within two years, the first plants capable of lifting well above the disturbed earth begin to make an appearance.

Able to tolerate the poorest soils, seemingly needing little more than moisture for growth, the fast-growing and short-lived aspens can establish themselves across a cleared area in a decade or less. In the faint shade of their scanty canopies sprout the first seedlings of a new, more lasting forest—perhaps oaks brought as acorns by squirrels, basswoods seeking to fill ample trunks with root-drawn water, jack pines, whose seeds are freed from their cones only by the heat of fire.

Not by coincidence does the aspen resemble a skeleton. It is truly the framework, the bone upon which nature constructs its most elegant of creations, a forest.

ℰℴ   ℭℛ

The Turtle and the Photographer

Nothing is quite as inviting as a day of sun after three days of cold and rain. It had been the sort of late April rain that washes away the last remnants of winter and leaves the world cleansed in preparation for the arrival of sping.

The trail I followed had been a road once, but no official motor traffic had passed along the route in fifty years. Two deep and winding ruts remained. Occasionally the tracks of an all-terrain vehicle or four-wheel-drive truck piloted by some exceptionally hardy (or, at least, foolhardy) soul marred the trail, but the old road mainly had been left to those who traveled on foot and whose destination and schedule were generally less than precise.

Roughly one-quarter mile in along the winding trail lay the most significant traces of human presence found in the area. In the early years of the century, a hydroelectric dam spanned the river, generating electricity for the nearby town. The dam was dynamited by some anonymous saboteur in 1930, and, some time after, it was completely removed from the river. An unnaturally straight stretch of rapids marks the location, along with an eerily shadowed trio of arches, former floodgates, removed from all but the faintest memories of their original use. On each bank of the river, crumbling stairways lead nowhere, and everywhere nearby, the visitor must clamber over massive slabs of concrete.

A deep ditch was cut into the north bank of the river in the days of the dam, forming a spillway through which excess water was diverted. Though the spillway was blocked off years ago, a portion of it remains as a backwater of the river, filled with stagnant water, which by summer's end is completely choked with algae. But in spring, the water lies cleared and freshened by snow melt. It is a haven for every sort of life, in particular the pair of wood ducks I hoped to capture on film, aided by a newly-purchased telephoto lens.

The wind chased its tail, lifting tiny vortices of fallen leaves from beneath the still-bare trees and tossing them high into the air. Beneath its breath, I heard the trilling voices of frogs, not the chorus that would become a constant background within a month, but a few soloists determined to make up in volume what they lacked in numbers. I had hoped the sound of the wind might screen my footsteps from the duck's hearing. A few seconds later, I caught sight of two pairs of desperately flapping wings headed away from me.

I decided to have a look at the old spillway anyway, hoping I could find a place to set up my camera and wait in hiding for the ducks to return. Perhaps some other picture-worthy subject might be found in or around the shadowy waters. Moving quietly, trying to cause as little commotion as possible, I crept to the rim of the spillway.

On a fallen log protruding from the dark water sat an unexpected quarry. A painted turtle, known more commonly as

a mud turtle, reclined in a patch of sunlight, looking as if it had never welcomed anything more than the coming of spring. It was the first turtle I had seen that year—a worthy target for the new telephoto, albeit not the one for which I had hoped. I knew from experience that turtles could be quite wary but hoped that the still-cool water would have slowed this one's cold-blooded metabolism, possibly leaving it sluggish enough for me to approach within picture range.

I carefully set down my equipment, unfolding my tripod without a sound and removed the wide-angle lens I had been carrying, replacing it with the much heavier telephoto. The lens locked into place with a small click, and the turtle slipped into the water with a resounding *plop!*

Whether turtles are capable of laughter, I do not know. I am inclined to think this one giggled as it submerged. I waited nearly an hour for it to return to the log, to no avail. Evidently the turtle and the wood ducks were in communication, for the ducks did not return either.

When the weather warms, I plan to give the old spillway another try. The wood ducks will have moved on by them, but turtles remain through the summer. Perhaps if I can catch one out on a still, sluggishly hot day, it will be sleepy enough to let me get close enough for a picture.

80   CR

A Sprouting of Spring

Each year holds a moment, a single small and often barely remembered incident revealing spring's arrival. The sound of water dripping from melting icicles or the first sunrise to climb from behind swelling, fluffy cumulus. A flock of geese winging north or the appearance of yellow feathers among the goldfinch's olive-drab winter plumage. Spring may come while one wanders the remotest wilderness or, as it did for me one year, while crossing the asphalt parking lot of a small-town bank.

Winter is a time of hunger; it is not merely by chance that many people gain weight during the long nights and forbidding temperatures of what often seems the longest season. But food satisfies only one hunger. In winter, I am especially prone to the eye's hunger for color. Winter's palette is limited: white, grey, brown, the occasional flash of blue from open water or a cold, clear sky. My eyes starve for green, the color of life. The first trace of it, however tiny, draws my eyes like few other things on earth.

The snow had gone several weeks before. Rain had washed away what rising temperatures had failed to melt. The forest stood as if waiting, a bundle of sticks displaying little promise of what sun and moisture would bring to their dry limbs in a few weeks. Open areas were expanses of dead grass sodden by rain and melting snow, flecked with months of wind-blown dust and the remains of snow mold, some of it already beginning to decay.

Surrounded by lifeless brown while my eyes sought green, winter remained close about my spirit. The dark, frozen season seemed determined to keep its hold on me even though it had gone from the world. Several trips into the woods, camera in hand, had revealed nothing of interest. One day, abandoning the idea of attempting photography, I headed into town to run some errands. The forest surrounding my home, so often a source of countless impressions, seemingly had none left to give me. During the six-mile trip to town, I took little notice of the area through which I passed.

There was no way I could have known that spring was at last about to find me. But it did.

The moment came during a walk along a row of buildings, a shortcut that led me through the parking lot of one of the local banks. The surface of the asphalt was dry, while the ground beneath fields and the dormant forest remained sodden. Absorbing the heat of the sun, the earth beneath the asphalt had warmed. While patches of frost-hardened ground could still be found in countless shaded areas in woods and field, the soil beneath the parking lot had long since thawed.

From a crack in the parking lot's surface, a silent testament to the warmth had emerged. The long-sought flash of green rose from the earth to banish the months of snow and darkness.

It was little enough to look at on first glance. A few ten-

tative, toothed leaves arranged sparsely along a stem little more than an inch high, a stem frail from the struggle of growing in the confines of the crack and under the still-limited sunlight of the early season. A seed, deposited in the crack by random whim, had sprouted some days earlier. From the tiny gap through the man-made world, a plant rose. It was gill-over-the-ground, the nearly indestructible bane of gardeners and land-scapers more commonly known as Creeping Charlie.

I bent to touch it. The leaves were soft; plucked and crushed, one of them gave off a heady, mint-like scent. Though faint as the leaf was small, the smell was spicy, exotic, of distant, wonderful and perhaps even magical places. To one whose spirit had been trapped in a world from which everything warm and gentle had for so long been excluded, smothered, buried by snow and ice, the sight of green and marvelous scent nearly shocked my system.

I have pulled and grubbed countless handfuls of Creeping Charlie from my yard and garden, sprayed various toxic chemicals around building foundations in largely vain attempts to keep it at bay. Had I passed by the tiny specimen in the bank parking lot at a later date or found it elsewhere in the middle of a group of plants, it would have made no real impression on me. The chances are that I would not have noticed it. If I had, my response probably would have been one of disdain, even disgust.

But in the moments I crouched beside the fragile thing and plucked one of its tiny leaves, it was the most beautiful living creation in the world. I had responded to the presence of others of its species with hoe and herbicide and more than a few curses. And, in return, the Creeping Charlie gave me spring.

℘   ℃

From Tiny Acorns

I stood in the shade of a high sandstone cliff, on a winding trail through massive slabs of fallen stone beside the shore of a placid river. The trail often led over, not around, the huge, fractured boulders; the going was treacherous. Though much of the ground underfoot was solid rock, the trail passed through areas of slick mud and loose gravel. Each step had to be taken with care to avoid countless deep fissures.

Beside me, the lower part of the cliff had fallen away. A small spring, which dampened the ground nearby, had eroded the cliff base still further. Beneath the overhang, a small cave had formed, its entrance wreathed in hoary moss and lichens. The beam of my small flashlight failed to penetrate the cave's limits. Bowing my head to clear the overhang, I ducked inside in search of whatever might be found there.

Solid rock lay beneath my feet and above my head. Aware that the chamber had been formed by the collapse of hundreds of tons of surrounding rock and that such collapses undoubtedly recurred from time to time, I did not want to linger. The rear of the cave proved to be less than fifty feet from the entrance, so exploration would not take long.

Along the stone floor at one edge of the "room" in which I stood, a fracture perhaps six inches wide ran all the way to the rock face at the rear. This crack was filled with a mixture of soil and rotten vegetation that had been blown, washed, or otherwise found its way into the space. Nothing would ever grow here, I thought. Not in this perpetual night.

But as I swung the beam of my flashlight along the crack, I noticed that something indeed did grow there. Atop the deposited soil lay an acorn that had found its way into the chamber either through the whim of the elements or a passing

13

squirrel. From one end of the acorn, a pale root had emerged, plunging into the soil in the crack. Just above the root, the frail beginnings of a stem rose hopefully toward my light.

An acorn consists of food intended to support the initial growth of the oak germ nestled inside. When that food is consumed, the infant oak must find sunlight or die. To a green plant, light is as essential as fertile soil.

Close examination of the sprouting acorn revealed that the shell from which the root and tiny stem had emerged was nearly empty, its supply of food nearly exhausted. The stem, which bore at its top the tiniest buds of potential leaves, was a sickly white, devoid of the chlorophyll that, in the presence of sunlight, would have manufactured sugar to feed the young oak. Here in the darkness, the chlorophyll had not been stimulated to develop.

This hopeless growth could continue for a few days more. The stem might lengthen; perhaps a pair of colorless leaves begin to open. But when the last of the seed food encased in the acorn's shell was exhausted, the tiny oak would die. It was dying as I looked upon it. As I write this, it has undoubtedly rotted and become part of the barren soil in the crack.

The cave floor was wet and slippery, the air in the chamber stagnant, a reminder that this was as much an alien place for me as it was for the pitiful would-be oak tree. I shivered, only partially from the cold. A few careful steps brought me out of the cave and back into the warm afternoon, but it was some time before the chill of the cave left me.

Caves are not lifeless places. Bats and snakes find comfortable shelters there; insects and fish abound in deep grottos never exposed to sunlight. The former are but visitors, the latter usually eyeless and colorless. Sight and color belong to the world of light, the world to which both the acorn and I belonged. I could leave the cave behind; the acorn, alas, was bound by its roots to the darkness.

෩　෨

On Being a Tree

Spring often blows into Minnesota on the back of a strong wind. The wind that had brought the first thunderstorms of the year during the previous night had long since carried its cloudy burden far away, leaving only an occasional puff of cumulus to screen the sun. But the wind remained, in sufficient strength to set still-bare aspens to waving and peel fallen leaves from the matted forest floor, scattering them far and wide.

I had come in search of wildflowers, a search that had produced few results. The few blossoms I found were tiny and tentative, the odd hepatica or spring beauty, occasional clusters of three leaves centered by the paling bud that would become a large-flowered trillium in a week or so. What I had found seemed best viewed by creatures with eyes closer to the ground than mine.

The combined effects of hours of walking and the sunny afternoon made me terribly sleepy, and the camera equipment dangling from my neck and shoulders grew heavier, until I had no desire to carry it farther. A massive white oak tree at the top of a small rise provided an excuse to linger.

A century or more old, gnarled with each of the winters it had known and, still almost budless, seemingly reluctant to leave the most recent one behind, the oak surveyed an expanse of aspen and mixed, brushy undergrowth. Massive roots sprawled outward like straining fingers reaching far from the trunk in search of what nutrition they could find in five inches of topsoil. Two such roots had grown into the arms of a perfect, natural chair, the back formed by the formidable trunk of the oak and the seat by the earth itself. It was an invitation I could not resist.

I shrugged off the camera gear, plunked my back and backside down between the huge roots, and wriggled my spine and the back of my head into furrows in the bark, which seemed, after a few moments, not random but ready-made to hold them. My head had settled with my face upturned toward the sun; my eyes closed naturally. All around me fell silent.

I was not fully aware of what happened next until after the experience had passed. The cynic would say that I merely dozed or slipped briefly into that twilight of the human consciousness commonly called hypnosis. To be sure, I was tired and had little of importance occupying my mind, a set of conditions quite conducive to either state. And yet . . .

The pace of time altered, as if everything in motion was no longer of consequence, as if I had begun to exist on a scale where movement was too transient to be worthy of notice. Discomfort lurked in this sensation but only for the briefest moment.

Then anxiety gave way to the understanding that time really did not matter, that the dictates of wristwatch or schedule were also transient and, therefore, trivial. I no longer recalled when I had come to the forest, how long I had been

there, or when I might leave. Such things no longer concerned me.

The best possible role of any forest wanderer is that of observer, preferable in the sense that the primary alternative is to intrude. Few humans are able to attain the state of absolute observer. Most send waves of disturbance and alarm before them—crashing footsteps, light-hearted conversation with companions or self, swaying arms, and harsh, intrusive scent—as they enter the woods. What they observe is, at best, what lacks the ability or desire to flee.

I sensed now that I had become not merely an observer but an *element* of the scene surrounding me, an immobile and utterly inconspicuous bit-player in a strange and silent drama unfolding on a scale of centuries. The day did not matter; there would be others. I was here now; I had always been here, would always be here. I felt utterly patient and impassive, ancient and gnarled by countless winters and countless winds.

And then, with realization of the moment, the moment ended, and I was again a weary wanderer sitting under a tree on a windy afternoon. No reason existed to linger longer. I packed up my gear and went home. Only much later would I begin to feel shaken by what had occurred.

The moment was incredibly brief, taking far longer to describe than to experience. But I was left exhausted by its passing, shaken by the utter conviction that I, for some split second, had melded with the bole of the massive tree against which I sat. For that split second, I had seen through the unimaginably patient eyes of the ancient, gnarled oak tree.

ℰℴ   ℭ℞

An Encounter with Innocence

I had visited the place a week before and been disappointed. Winter keeps its watch a bit longer in the northern half of Minnesota, and spring requires more time to awaken fully. With a pack stuffed with camera equipment, I had set out in search of wildflowers, finding instead only a few tentative patches of green grass, clusters of immature leaves still struggling to pull free of the stems they embraced, the occasional feeble bud revealing the promise of a flower but still days away from opening. I did not stay long, and returned home almost without removing the camera from my pack.

What a difference a week of warmth and an inch of rain made! On returning, I found the forest floor richly carpeted with lush grass. Tiny mushrooms sprouted from fallen logs. Trillium buds had swelled to fully-flowered wonders, their brillant, white blossoms like stars somehow brought to earth and half hidden in the forest's semi-shadows. Purple and yellow violets clustered close around the bases of trees. And, in two spots, I found the glossy, embracing pairs of leaves from which would sprout the delicate lavender flower known as the stemless lady's-slipper.

I searched upward as well. In May, the oyster mushroom often sprouts from the wood of dead aspens, which were abundant in the area. Few gastronomical delights compare to fresh sliced mushrooms added to a stir-fry dish. Alas, after seaching the aspen trunks for some time, I saw no sign of the delicately shaped and delicious fungus. I decided to concentrate on the ground. Even so, I nearly missed what would become the highlight of the afternoon.

The color first alerted me, a shade of brown too warm and red to be a cluster of leaves or a log. As it registered at the corner of my eye, I froze. I had blundered past something. One learns to heed such sensations in the woods. On another occasion, what I can only describe as an inner voice had told me, quite suddenly, to stop in the middle of a field of grass. I did. Right where my next footfall would have landed lay a basketball-sized paper nest filled with crawling, bald-faced hornets.

What signaled me this time was not the voice of warning but that of curiosity. As I focused more closely on the patch of brown, I realized it was fur. A dead animal, I thought, perhaps a fox; I had seen tracks on previous visits indicating that such creatures could be found in the area. But then, as I turned toward the brown fur, it stirred slightly. A head, eyes, and prominent ears came into view. A newborn whitetail deer.

I froze in my tracks again, fearing that the slightest movement would frighten the fawn. But, when it seemed to take little notice of me, I moved closer. The fawn looked at me but did not move.

It reclined in the shade of a fallen log, surrounded in part by last year's dried grass, which, combined with the distinctive white spots on its coat, hid it almost completely from sight. It gazed at me with a wide-eyed innocence such as I have never before seen in any living creature. I was, almost certainly, the first human being it had ever seen.

I looked for the doe, which had undoubtedly hidden the fawn. There was no sign of her, and I was glad. An animal fearing for its offspring could be bad-tempered indeed, and the hooves of a whitetail were as sharp as knives. In all likelihood, the doe had concealed the fawn and gone off to feed, a common practice. Wanderers occasionally encountered fawns hidden in this manner and thought them orphaned. They were almost always wrong.

I watched the fawn for some minutes, taking a series of photographs and approaching briefly to within three feet of it. I did not touch it. I didn't want to make the transition from observer to intruder by doing that. The mere depositing of my alien scent could have serious consequences. That alone might terrify the doe into abandoning her fawn.

After a while, I moved quietly away, seeking to disturb the beautiful creature as little as possible. I have read since that the instinct of a newborn whitetail is to keep still if startled, since they are too frail to find safety in flight. But the fawn did not seem to fear me; at least it showed no sign I could interpret as fear. I wonder now, and try to remember, if I was ever so young that I did not know how to be afraid.

℘　℞

Looking at the Wind

I know a place where I can take a good look at the wind. It's called Norway Point, named for the red or "Norway" pines growing along its high, steep-banked contours. Familiars of the place simply call it the Point. A twisting peninsula jutting out roughly one quarter mile into the north end of a six-mile lake, perhaps one hundred yards across at its widest, Norway Point narrows as it extended into the lake, until, when its tip finally drops into water, it is barely fifty feet wide.

The red pines along the point form one of the few concentrated stands of such trees in the immediate area. Evergreen foliage once dominated the countryside, but, between the middle of the last century and the 1920s, lumber companies clear-cut most of the county. The present-day forest consists mainly of red and white oak, paper birch, and the occasional red or sugar maples that succeeded the aspens that followed the old-growth pines. One encounters lonely individual pines and spruce and occasional small clumps. A visit to any forested area will generally reveal a number of evergreen seedlings, signs that the old forest is reasserting itself and will someday return if left to its own devices.

The red pine is a particularly sturdy species, capable of surviving three hundred years or more. The sentinels that dot the stony ridge of Norway Point seem ancient indeed, some two feet or more in diameter at the base. The red pine is also noted for the straightness of its trunk, which led lumbermen to regard it as prime timber. But the Norway Point pines saw the loggers come and go and survived. Their numbers were too few, or the difficulty of cutting trees on the narrow, high-crowned peninsula too great, to make the task worthwhile.

The trees are survivors in another sense. Norway Point

21

has little topsoil. What is not solid rock is sand, gravel, and stones all mixed together by the glacier, dumped and shaped during the last ice age. The sparse grasses and occasional wild-flowers—harebells and bindweed in summer, little else in other seasons—are spindly from struggling to feed upon the dust of fallen needles, the main source of nutrients. The pines appear to have fought for every millimeter of their growth. Huge, gnarled roots twist above the ground where erosion exposed them, coiling at last into the earth like snakes returning to their burrows.

The wind, however, has done more to shape the trees than anything else. It carries the soil away from the roots even as they struggle to retain it. Norway Point is exposed to the elements on three sides. In my experience, the air has never been still there.

That wind, carrying dust and rain in summer and snow, sleet, and frost in winter, has clawed at each of the trees. Some trees cradle dead limbs on their most exposed side. Others lean fantastically, as if permanently drawing back from the relentless wind. Every tree is scarred, gnarled and battered by everything Minnesota weather can throw at it. Few, if any, display the proud, straight trunks that brought joy to the timber barons' eyes.

Several cabins have been built along the wider parts of the point in recent years, but the very tip is too narrow and exposed to allow construction, and it has been left to the wind. At that completely unprotected spot stands a single white ash. The species is uncommon in the area. And this specimen, as exposed as it could possibly be to the elements, struggling in the poorest of soils, is most uncommon indeed.

The ash is nearly dead—wind, frost, and quite possibly lightning having killed nearly half of its branches. Its trunk is twisted, its bark split in several places. Yet each spring, it sends forth another crop of leaves, a somewhat sparser crop each year, to be sure, but no less green than any of its predecessors. Life is a remarkable thing; it finds what hope it can and, from that, endures.

Not far from the base of the twisted ash, a deep depression mars the otherwise smooth slope of the point toward the water. Local legend has it that the pit marks the site of a meteor strike. More likely it was the work of others who knew the wind, the native people of the area, who used the site to winnow gathered wild rice from chaff. The point was once a popular place to search for arrowheads and other artifacts. Excavators digging the foundations of one of the cabins unearthed stone tools possibly thousands of years old.

Wild rice no longer grows in the lake, and it's quiet now at the end of Norway Point. Little attracts people or animals, and, aside from the occasional perching kingfisher or heron, the only movement and sound generally comes from the grass or the pine boughs nodding in the breeze.

There's a natural chair, carved from the hillside by erosion, at the end of the point. From time to time, I'll be there, having a good look at the wind through the eyes of the pines and the ash, through the memories of the rice winnowers and the others who came before, perhaps to look themselves.

ഓ ൙

Birds of a Feather

The only living elm trees in the area stood in our front yard. Three of a group of five lived, but one had begun to show yellow leaves. Bare branches betrayed the presence of the invading Dutch Elm Disease that would eventually take its life.

The arching branches of the elm are favored nest sites of Baltimore orioles. Their sack-like nests are intricately woven of twigs, grasses, and adhesive bits of cobweb. The elms held oriole nests each year. One year, the nest clung to a branch near the house. From the roof, or the unlikely vantage of the upstairs bathroom window, the orioles could be observed at close range.

I climbed to the roof one hot afternoon a few days after the orioles' four eggs had hatched. Neither the hatchlings nor their mother seemed disturbed by my presence. She covered the hatchlings with her warming body and, from time to time, left the nest to gather some scrap of food to bring to them. They held up their tiny beaks in silent pleas for food, more than once hoping to get it from me when the hen was absent.

The brilliant orange male was often about. Sometimes he brought food to the nest; on occasion, he eyed me for signs of threat. Mostly he sat on a nearby utility wire, letting the sun display his glowing plumage to best advantage, and he often sang his distinctive series of warbling notes. A beautiful song but one with a menacing purpose: a warning to other orioles that might approach his territory and family.

Though the shingles were uncomfortably hot, I lay on my stomach and gazed into the nest. The female oriole warmed her hatchlings. The male perched on the wire and sang.

A huge shadow crossed the yard. With a slow whisper of wing, a sharp-shinned hawk slipped from the sky and perched on the utility wire, perhaps fifty feet from the orioles' nest.

For a moment, all fell silent in the yard, instinct telling potential prey to keep still. But only for a moment. From the throat of the male oriole came a song I had never heard before, not its usual melodious call but a piercing shriek instantly apparent as alarm. Again and again came the call, and I realized that the oriole feared for the nest and hatchlings.

The call was taken up from the far side of the yard. Another male oriole, encroaching on the first's territory, landed in a nearby tree and began to shriek the same desperate sound. Two more orioles arrived. Perching at opposite corners of the yard, they too began the piercing alarm call. Meanwhile, the hawk stayed perched on the wire.

Other calls began, similar but different in tone, for they came from different throats. Two bluejays and a hairy woodpecker flapped to the branches of a nearby pine and joined the chorus. Others, unseen, lurked in the forest that surrounded the yard. The noise level was terrific, the message obvious: fear of the hawk and an overwhelming desire to drive it away.

Quickly as it had begun, the stand-off ended. In the unconcerned manner of raptors, the hawk spread its wings, lofted into the air and flapped out of sight. The racket stopped as if by command. The visiting oriole reinforcements disappeared almost immediately. The bluejays went next, then the woodpecker. Finally, all was peaceful again for the pair of orioles.

The male oriole spent hours each day in warning away others of his kind. But when his nest and hatchlings were threatened, not only were the others welcome but apparently expected. They came, along with others. Despite differences, despite the walls that nearly all living creatures erect around themselves, boundaries tend to fall when a threat arrives. Nothing brings living things together like the need for a helping hand—or, as in this case, a helping song.

ℰ   ℭ

Too Far Upstream

The previous week had brought rain in near-record amounts. Summer eased in soggily, accompanied by flooded fields, heavy, humid days, and a lush growth of vegetation from every spot that could support it. Many tilled fields, ironically, remained almost bare. In some, seed had been washed from the soil or drowned before it could sprout. Other fields lay unplanted, the ground too soft to support machinery.

The month of June saw the limbs of my family's orchard already beginning to bend under a dangerously heavy load of green apples. Apple trees generally drop some of their fruit as soon as the weather begins to turn dry, adjusting the weight of the branches to what they can bear, strengthening the remainder by discarding the weak or poorly-attached. In that wet year, the apples held, swelling far byond their usual June size. Branches would snap under the weight of ripening fruit by summer's end.

With the rain had come a week of disappointments and anxieties—professional setbacks, a family quarrel, a painful reminder of a long-ago failed romance. Troubled, I sought distraction in small errands, with little success. But on a hot afternoon, the day after a thunderstorm had first washed the grass, then pounded it flat to the earth, one such errand brought me to the far end of the orchard.

The south portion of the orchard followed a slope that edged off into the woods bordering the planted area, then steepened to become one bank of a ravine following a twisted track through the forest to the lake perhaps five hundred feed away. The ravine drained a small swamp just south of the orchard, separated from it by a gravel driveway but connected to the ravine by a steel culvert. To the east was another swamp, held at bay by an unpaved road but joined to the smaller wetland by a similar corrugated metal pipe.

The swamps filled with each snow melt, and, for several weeks each year, the ravine ran as a stream, carrying the silt-laden remains of winter from the land. In a typical year, however, the water stopped running long before the first week of June, the swamps retaining sufficient moisture to keep the cat-tails alive and provide a refuge for frogs but only rarely enough to attract the eye with a flash of reflected sun on water beneath the reeds. That year, however, the ravine still flowed with sur-plus rainfall, though July was little more than a week away, and the swamps remained swollen with moisture. Frogs sang in chorus day and night, as if delighted by the abundance.

A faint gurgling came from the culvert under the drive-way, the sound of the water struggling through it. It was a pleasant sound, a soft accompaniment to the frogs, reassuring in its continuity. The preceding three years had known drought, and the sound of running water had become almost unfamiliar.

I had planted no crops that could be washed away by the recent rains and was not seriously troubled by the record mos-quito hatch, which had come in the wake of an abundance of standing water.

To me the sound of running water is the sound of life. That afternoon, I needed to be reminded of life, of the goodness of life, of anything but the events that had brought me to the slope south of the orchard. I knew not what I sought there, only that I sought, and that it was for something far beyond the triv-ial errand—my avowed purpose—which had long since drifted from memory.

Quite suddenly a loud splash came from one end of the driveway culvert, the sound of something large and living strik-ing the water. From behind the screen of tall grass that hid the mouth of the culvert, a sheet of spray rose into the air. The sound stopped me in my tracks.

I could imagine no good reason for anything to be in the culvert, half-filled as it was with nearly a foot of water. There seemed little possibility that anything likely to choose such a refuge would be a creature I cared to meet face to face. It was big; the sound had told me that.

My first thought was that a raccoon or a skunk—perhaps even a woodchuck—had sought out the shadows of the pipe as a refuge from the heat, unlikely prospect though that was. All those animals were equipped with sharp teeth and the potential for disagreeable behavior. Curiosity, however, would not let me ignore the splash. Few occurrences cry out more strongly for explanation than those both unexpected and seemingly inexplicable.

I tossed a few pebbles into the tall grass near the mouth of the culvert. They produced sufficient racket, I presumed, to provoke further movement from the unknown animal and possibly tempt it into showing its face. I waited, but as the splashes of the pebbles died away, the only lingering sound was the continuing gurgling of water. The mysterious noisemaker had either departed or hidden inside the pipe. I remained reluctant to investigate closely. I shortly returned to the house.

ℬ　ℬ　ℭ　ℭ

The day passed in humid sluggishness, signs of relief only arriving as the sun approached the horizon. My continuing seach for distraction brought me outdoors again, this time for a walk down the gravel road in front of the house.

There was no wind. The air, though beginning to cool, was lifeless and unpleasant in the lungs, giving little sense of nourishment in passing through them. Beside the road as it began to dip toward the twin swamps, a large clump of sweet clover swelled in full flower. It smelled fresh and living and new, was soft and enviably cool to the touch. I wanted to bury my face in its sweetness, but, struck by anxiety that an onlooker might take unwelcome notice of such a childish display, I restrained myself and moved on.

As I approached the stretch of road passing between the swamps, I thought I sensed a note of discontent in the frogs' nighttime chorus, perhaps anxiety at my approach or, I allowed myself to fancy, displeasure at the heat. Here, water gurgled under the road as well, and, with the coming of nightfall, the hum of insects rose in every direction.

Then, this time from the road culvert, came a splash like I had heard earlier in the day. It seemed louder than before but, then, so did the gravel under my boots and the surrounding wings of countless mosquitoes. It was, after all, an extremely still summer evening.

I did not catch sight of the splash of water this time, but the reeds and grasses beside the mouth of the culvert stirred slightly. Something living moved about there, and I was determined to see what it was.

Again, caution dictated my first efforts. I tossed a few small stones into the area around the culvert's mouth, hoping to drive the unknown creature into the open. As before, no response. And so, this time, my curiosity drove me onward. Walking with small steps as quietly as possible, I moved to the edge of the road, where the culvert emerged, and pushed back the tall grass that hid its mouth from sight.

Barely able to submerge completely in the shallow water but with gills moving easily in the oxygen-rich current, a large common carp floated, logy and fat, well-fed, no doubt, on insects like the one it had almost certainly just caught, causing the splash that had caught my attention.

The rain had brought it, of course. Runoff had kept the ravine swollen with water long past the usual time, well into the spawning season of the carp, a season during which females sought out shallows in which to join with males of their kind, laying up to a million eggs each. The struggle against the current in the ravine must have been difficult indeed, but it had brought the carp to a shallow, which must have seemed an appropriate place. There it had waited, probably frequenting the culverts for their shade and slightly deeper water, hoping for the arrival of a mate.

It would, in all likelihood, wait in vain. That even one carp could find its way so far up a temporary feeder of the lake was difficult to accept even when undeniable proof tread water only a few feet away. I could not imagine another making the same journey and the same mistake.

The swamp was not a fit home for a gill-breather; most of the water would drain away within a few weeks. Already the water level in the ravine flowing out of the wetland had dropped so much that it was highly unlikely that the carp could make its way back to the lake. With each passing day the sun would grow hotter, the land drier and the water lower. The swamp would become stagnant, and, not long after that, one of my evening walks would be marked by the unmistakable smell of dead fish.

The carp enjoys little respect from those who encounter it. Efforts have been made in many areas to eradicate it, and an angler hooking one by mistake (for few would deliberately fish for them) is far more likely to throw this catch on shore to rot than carry it home. But, as I looked down at the solitary specimen, who could not know the inevitability of her fate, I felt a sudden and intense kinship and a desire to help. She had raised herself to nobility in my eyes through her foolishness, and I wished I had something to offer her for her troubles beyond the promise of a slow death in the drying swamp.

Certain members of every species are driven to single-minded pursuit of a goal, ignoring the obstacles that lie before it. Such individuals inevitably fail to realize that the end result is far less likely to be the foot of the rainbow as a fate for which the journey has left them completely unprepared, and from which there may be no escape. Some manage to adapt; others cannot, facing a metaphorical or actual suffocation in stinking mud.

The carp would certainly not be the first creature to die for her dreams, nor the last to throw her life away in pursuit of a mate. All too often, we struggle too far upstream in pursuit of something that is unlikely to be there. Yet we continue to idolize those few who succeed, and romanticize the legions who perish.

I wished I could speak to the carp, to give warning while sufficient water remained in the ravine to make return to the lake possible, if barely so. I wished for a net, that I might return the errant creature to the lake myself. In the end, I could only comfort myself with the thought that even if intervention were possible, the fish might well resent my efforts. She had brought herself to a certain end on the strength of her own efforts, and, if that end was not to be a happy one, the journey to it was at least the most ambitious of her lifetime. Who was I to interfere? I tried to smile and turned away.

ॐ   ॐ

One Small Sight, One Soft Sound

Two fields east of my home stands a sprawling white oak, an ancient specimen with a massive, forked trunk and limbs spreading wide into branches nearly touching the ground with the tips of their smallest twigs. Years ago, someone nailed crude rungs to the trunk and fixed a plywood platform between the three main forks of the trunk about ten feet from the ground, presumably for use as a deer stand. But during the fifty weeks of the year when the deer season is closed, this platform is one of the finest places I know to watch the sun set.

Many is the summer evening I've perched on the platform, sticky with sweat from the walk to the base of the tree and reeking of Muskol (mosquitoes, unfortunately, love to climb trees, too), relishing the deep, surrounding shade found nowhere but in the canopy of an ancient oak.

A human being walking quickly through any wild area is an intruder frightening nearby wildlife into immobility. Silence surrounds the oak each time I approach. But, in moments, this cautious quiet gives way to the subtle movements and occasionally frenzied activity of an evening forest, for a person sitting quietly in a tree is close to invisible. Chipmunks, grey squirrels, and a woodchuck have scaled the oak during several of my visits, passing within inches of me without noticing my presence. On another occasion, a bat emerged from a hole in the tree some distance above my head and, with a chorus of irritated clicking squeaks, set about its night-long task of consuming its weight in insects.

The oak stands in a thin strip of brushy forest that forms the boundary between two large fields, which, depending on the year, are planted in corn or alfalfa. Both crops are attractive fodder for deer, and an hour spent in the oak on a summer evening often leads to the sighting of one or more whitetails. One such evening climaxed with a remarkable moment.

Arriving at the tree about half an hour before sunset, I had barely settled myself into a comfortable position on the platform when the first deer, a doe accompanied by two young fawns whose coats still showed traces of the white camouflaging spots of their infancy, wandered into the field. From about fifty yards away, on an evening with little air movement, I watched as they began to feed. I was amazed, as I have been time and again, that the deer were as silent as the evening. No sound arose from their slow, tentative footsteps, nor did any sort of communication pass between them. The fawns moved as

if directed by their mother, bowing to eat when she did, moving again when she did, presumably in imitation of her. All else was almost utter silence.

As I watched them, I became aware of a new presence just beneath me and the lower branches of the oak. When I turned to look, slowly and carefully so as not to make any noise that might intrude on the scene, I saw another whitetail, this one a buck with magnificent velvet antlers. He passed almost directly beneath me. As he did so, a sound reached my ears, the tiniest of whispers from the grass as each of his hooves touched the earth.

Just as the buck passed under the oak, he stopped, and I froze, not daring to breathe for fear of alerting him. But, to the buck, I was quite invisible. As I watched, he bowed his head to snatch a clump of grass from the forest floor.

In that moment, I heard a wonderful thing: the sound of the buck chewing his mouthful of grass and swallowing.

He moved on then, as slowly and in near silence as he had come. In a few moments, the brush, gathering shadows, and low-hanging branches of the oak hid him from my sight. I did not see him again.

Come November, the platform on the ancient oak will be occupied by a hunter, someone also looking for deer, but seeing them only as a source of food or sport. Lest anyone should wonder, I have no quarrel with this. Indeed, I have ventured into the forest for such reasons myself. But, on that hot July evening, I found a far greater pleasure in seeing—and hearing—the buck eat than I could ever have derived from feeding on him.

෨ ෬

The Pride of the Carnivore

When I was a child, I hated to see animals eat. Wild animals, I mean, of the sort that populated the documentaries on television during the dinner hour on weekends when there was no football. Weekends when families, including my own, often partook of the dubious luxury of eating in front of the TV. Often my family's living room was transformed into a Wild Kingdom for the duration of the evening meal.

As a child, more than one meal was utterly ruined for me by this weekly "treat." I don't know how anyone could enjoy a hamburger while lions stripped their prey of its intestines, or penguins regurgitated for the benefit of their young. I know I found it impossible. I often wondered why producers of such documentaries insisted on including such material, why they could not instead concentrate on the beauty of wild things, the sort of beauty that, even in early childhood, I had begun to appreciate through visits to the local zoo. Zoos displayed predators but no prey with them, and, for those creatures requiring meat in their diets, the food was generally kept out of public sight.

Humans rarely take great displeasure in the sight of a fellow human eating, provided that the proprieties of etiquette are observed. On reflection, this might be because our food is so often separated from its original source. The head, feathers, and entrails of a chicken are removed and disposed of by some faceless individual possibly hundreds of miles from where the meat is consumed. And is the imagination truly able to conceive that the cold, diluted blood in the bottom of a package of steaks once flowed warm and living through throbbing veins? When I was a child, I did not think of such things. I only knew I could not bear to see animals eating on television.

This sensibility would change quite abruptly on a still summer day during an afternoon forest walk. When in my middle twenties—and in the middle of July—I found myself in dense forest crossed by an old roadbed that followed the course of a fair-sized river.

Mid-summer is the worst time in Minnesota for mosquitoes and other biting insects, but the best for foliage. I often walk barefoot in the forest in summer, enjoying the sensation of intimate contact with the place I explored. But when the undergrowth thickens to the point that my feet become invisible, I discontinue the practice. I have never been able to escape the thought that something horrible might lie unseen just beneath my next unprotected footstep.

The temperature that July afternoon hovered in the high eighties, and every leaf, every blade of grass seemed to sweat moisture. The air was sluggish with dampness and the full, warm pungency of greenery. A swarm of mosquitoes pursued me, but the bottle of insect repellent remained in my pocket. Sweat washed most of it away almost as quickly as I applied it, and I had long since given it up. The smell of the stuff bothered me more than it seemed to bother July mosquitoes.

No species on earth can speak the language of another. But, since the vocabulary of the wild is limited, touching only upon basic necessities and urgencies, serious translation skills are rarely required. What came to my ears, unexpected and disconcertingly near, could have only one meaning in any language. It was a series of high-pitched squeaks, almost painfully loud and at times approaching the upper frequency limits of my hearing. The message was undeniable: it was a scream of mortal fear.

It did not occur to me until much later that the cries might be the result of an assault by an animal possessing large teeth and claws with no qualms about using them. The squeaking came from a clump of grass about twenty feet ahead of me, and I determined without hesitation to see what the commotion was about. I hurried toward the clump of grass, reached down to brush it aside. As I did, the squeaks faded and stopped.

I did not realize until they found their voices again that

every living creature in the area—the usual chorus of birds, frogs, and insects that are the continual background to a summer streamside forest—had fallen silent, the basic response to a threat in the wild. But, as the squeaks stopped and I drew back the grass concealing their source, first one, then another tentative voice began again as the bolder animals decided that the sudden quiet marked the passing of any immediate danger. It was some time, however, before the chorus sang at full strength again.

Beneath the clump of grass lay a common garter snake, perhaps two feet in length, a veteran of a recent skin-shedding as seen by the glossiness of its deep olive, five-banded skin. It was probably female by its size. The snake sprawled in a half-coil, its jaws dislocated and stretched almost absurdly to accommodate a burden nearly twice the diameter of its head. Protruding from those jaws were the wildly kicking hindquarters of a common field mouse. Silenced and suffocating but still struggling, the mouse's efforts seemed all the more hopeless for the fact that the snake appeared utterly impassive, at least uncaring if not utterly oblivious to them.

In my childhood, such a sight, even observed vicariously through a cold television eye, would have sent me rushing from the room, quite possibly fighting an impulse to retch. But, facing the living reality for the first time, I stared, utterly fascinated, as the hind legs of the mouse slowed and stilled, as the snake strained to swallow it bit by bit, as the legs finally disappeared and only the tail protruded. Then even the tail was gone, and the mouse, which had caught my ear with its dying scream, was only a swelling that made its way millimeter by millimeter along the body of the snake.

The straining reptile's mouth still gaped, and the snake looked up at me with the oddly staring eyes of its kind. With the burden in its gullet, the snake could barely move, and perhaps it feared I might attempt to steal its hard-won meal. In my childhoood, I might well have been tempted to try.

But now my heart swelled with an unexpected, primitive warmth, as if I had witnessed the taking of some rare and deeply profound sacrament, something infinitely beyond the simple reality that the snake had been hungry and the mouse had been there to be eaten. Or, perhaps, for the first time, the beginnings of understanding and acceptance of that simple reality awakened within me.

I watched for a long time, lingering well after nothing new could be seen, and the heat, humidity, and ever-gathering mosquitoes made remaining any longer undesirable. I released the clump of grass, restoring the garter snake's hiding place. It seemed to take no notice, lying quite still with its eyes open, their slitted pupils gazing upon nothing in particular. By that time, it may well have been asleep. But those eyes still gleamed with something primeval and profound, the pride of the carvnivore in slaking its hunger, the sense of rising strength in the flesh that comes of feeding on other flesh.

I left the forest that day freed of one burden: since then, I have never been troubled by the sight of wild things feeding, whether on television or directly before my eyes. I gained instead a possibly greater burden. For, while no human being consumes its meat while it's still living, nonetheless, for every bite we take, a life must also be taken. It is a deep and ancient responsibility, one that some, on becoming aware of it, are unable to bear. These turn away from the eating of meat.

For my own part, when I eat meat, I sometimes think of the eyes of the snake and of how they betrayed no trace of anything that, by any stretch of the imagination, could be construed as a display of emotion. But, at the same time, I am grateful that I never saw the eyes of the mouse.

ℰℴ ℂℛ

Flying between the Cracks

Under the lid of a gas grill, I once found a reminder of one of nature's greatest skills, adaptation. This may seem a strange place to find such a lesson, and, in retrospect, I find it incongruous that I should encounter it in such a location. I harbor a vague but long-standing dislike for gas grills. Something of the primitive in me, I guess. If I want to cook with fire, I prefer to do it the old-fashioned way.

The day had passed in the company of a recent acquaintance, as we had spent a series of hours informally discovering a world washed by heavy overnight rains. In the sluggish hours of an unseasonably hot afternoon, we sat on the porch and gazed through an atmosphere dancing with heat and moisture.

A house wren, surely one of the most hyperactive of birds, had perched on a nearby lilac branch and sat there berating us. That it was instinctively afraid of us, as most wild creatures are of any human, however well-intentioned, was obvious. What was not clear was its reason for remaining nearby, when flight would have seemed the easiest expedient.

As I pondered the tiny bird's determination to hold its ground, my eyes hit upon the solution to the small mystery. At the edge of the yard stood a gas grill, removed from winter storage some weeks before but as yet unused. From a narrow vent on one side of the lid protruded several small twigs. No good reason existed for twigs to be inside the grill. Their presence, coupled with that of the wren perched and chattering angrily a few feet away, however, revealed the reason.

Under the lid of the grill sat a haphazardly constructed mound of twigs, perhaps six inches high and slightly less across. A carefully formed, cup-shaped depression lined with soft grasses and feathers had been set into the top of the mound of twigs. Neatly centered in the cup, like pearls laid out upon a jeweller's velvet, lay three eggs, glossy white but heavily speckled with brown.

House wrens typically laid five to eight eggs, so more likely would come. I carefully closed the top of the grill, and my friend and I retreated sufficiently that our presence would no longer disturb the tiny mother. Later we lettered and placed a sign on the grill commanding that it be neither moved nor lit.

The house wren, so my field guide informed me, is noted for choosing eccentric nesting sites. Even the pockets of clothing hung out on the line to dry have been selected at times. Practically speaking, the pockets of line-drying laundry provide poor sites for nests. From the same perspective, however, the gas grill was a perfect spot. The lid excluded rain, the narrow vents, predators. All the wren needed to insure the safety of its brood was a gas grill owner willing to forgo outdoor cooking

until the brood had hatched, grown, and moved on. My friend was such a person.

Those who champion the cause of nature fashionably decry what people often choose to call "progress": endless acres of asphalt, countless towers erected before the horizon. Too easily such things are seen only as barriers between humanity and the natural world. We forget all too often that every building has its attics, every pavement its cracks. Inquisitive life, provided it is not purposefully and violently excluded, can find its way into and thrive in such places. Earthworms often find their way through cracks in asphalt parking lots and suffer when the pavement becomes a lifeless desert with the passing of rain. But peregrine falcons gratefully choose the ledges of skyscrapers for their aeries, and a tiny house wren once found shelter for a clutch of eggs beneath the lid of a gas grill.

Through some such metaphorical gaps in the world of the dinosaurs came the mammals and eventually ourselves. Now we in our turn leave cracks through which other species escape into our world. We have endured. So shall they.

৯০   ০৪

The Monster

During much of my childhood, I wished I could see a monster. Not a movie monster—not the jerky, half-humorous caricatures of late-night TV—but a real monster, live and in the flesh. One afternoon I did, and, to this day, there are times when I wish I had not.

It was during a week-long visit to my grandfather's 120-acre farm in the year I turned ten. Summer had begun to grow old; foliage no longer seemed new, displayed a curious, "settled" appearance. The thunderstorm season had ended, leaving behind long days of still, humid heat. The atmosphere quivered with moisture, but the leaves of every tree were dulled by a haze that resembled, and may have been, dust.

Even one with little imagination might have thought that the land was becoming bored, and midway through my visit, alone six miles from town and the company of anyone my own age, boredom had found me as well. The largest tree had been climbed, the farthest reaches of the fields walked, the darkest recesses of the barn explored. I had twice gone fishing and once attempted swimming before catching sight of a crayfish, which had frightened me from the water. The lawn had been mowed, and I had read all the available books that interested me.

In the words of my grandfather—who considered every rodent to be nothing more than a rat in slightly different clothing—there was a "plague of chipmunks" that year. They were on every woodpile and fallen log, scuttling along the foundations of the garage and rustling, unseen, in the shadows of the granary. Bait and traps had done nothing to decrease the population. Perhaps as much in the hope of keeping me busy as anything else, my grandfather offered me a nickel for every dead chipmunk I could bring him. The days when one could buy a candy

bar for a nickel were gone, but, nonetheless, the sum was irresistible, and the countryside seemingly crawling with chipmunks.

The means by which I was supposed to dispatch as
many of the unfortunate creatures as possible was simple and
readily available. The year before I had learned to shoot a .22-
caliber air rifle, a weapon of near-antique vintage that was kept
in the hall closet, along with a box of lead pellets. I was so small
and the action of the gun so stiff that every ounce of strength
from both hands was required to pump the gun up to the needed pressure. But once I had loaded it, an effort that often
required several minutes, I was a crack shot to the limit of the
range of the aging gun and its open sights, perhaps twenty-five
yards.

Chipmunks are relatively bold creatures, prone to perching in sunlit places, of which there were many in the lightly-
wooded pasture below the barn. This fatal habit allowed me to
bag half a dozen within an hour, most of them relatively
humanely. I collected the tiny corpses and set them at the base
of a prominent oak, there to be collected at the end of the afternoon's "sport" and taken to my grandfather for the promised
reward.

In time, I gathered my booty together, grasping the
small, furry bodies by their tails and preparing to carry them to
the house. Then I took a closer look at what I clutched tightly
in my hand. And I saw movement where there should be nothing moving.

It was only a flicker detected at the edge of my vision, but
it drove hard into a sensitive corner of my mind and released
an immediate and intense, though not at first understood, horror. My arm spasmed; I threw the dead chipmunks far from me
with an exclamation of disgust.

At first the horror was only a sensation without cause
beyond a vague impression that I had placed my hand near
something disgusting, possibly even touched it without knowing. But that was sufficient to make me wipe my hands thoroughly on the thick pasture grass, desperate to rub away any
lingering trace of the terrible uncertainty. I looked at the scat-

tered bodies of the chipmunks I had shot, determined not to pick them up.

But as several minutes passed, my pulse slowed, and my hands stopped shaking. I felt increasingly foolish for reacting so when I did not even know why. And thoughts of losing the promised thirty cents began to win out over disgust. I went over to the dead chipmunks and picked them up, carefully, one at a time. Until I came to the one which had caused me to throw the lot away.

Beneath the tail of the chipmunk, something was emerging. It was black, glossy with moisture, and what seemed to be its head wobbled and revolved as it struggled to free itself from the imprisoning corpse. Recollection is that it seemed to be about the size of my thumb, but my thumb was considerably smaller then. In any case, the creature—for it was obviously alive—was large enough to be horrible far beyond the understanding of a ten-year-old boy.

Despite immediate revulsion, I stared for some time as the thing dragged a bit more of itself into the world. It was vaguely similar in shape to a caterpillar, lumpy and displaying what looked like rows of stubby, unfinished-looking legs. I saw no eyes, only a series of proturberances that looked as if they might grip and burrow into anything they touched. And a head—if it was indeed a head—that spiralled endlessly about as if seeking something from which to draw food.

I could not bear to pick up the chipmunk. My stomach was beginning to churn, and the dead chipmunks in my hand seemed increasingly unwelcome there as fear began to rise that one or more might contain a similar horror. I ran with lunch rising in my throat and five furry bodies in my hand, dropping them beside a tree in front of the house, trying to forget what I had seen but knowing I never would.

The promise of a nickel would eventually lead me back. With a shovel in hand, for the thought of touching either the chipmunk or the thing that was emerging from it made my skin crawl, I returned about an hour later to where the chipmunk lay. Carefully, I slid it onto the shovel and lifted it from the earth. And horror gripped me once again.

The monster had emerged from the chipmunk. It lay in the grass, its stumpy leg-like appendages waving as if clawing at the earth, and its head (for it seemed more apparently a head now) still weaving back and forth, occasionally rotating as if scanning for prey. The thing rolled on the earth; black, wet, and seemingly desperate for sustenance of a sort I could not and dared not imagine.

I was still carrying the air gun. It was fully pumped and loaded. I set the muzzle perhaps an inch from the writhing horror and pulled the trigger.

When I looked again, the monster was gone.

Since those days, I have had several passing acquaintances with the study of biology and once toured the veterinary department of a major university. I have seen the nightmares that float sterilized in formaldehyde jars and Petri dishes, peered at the named horrors that creep beneath the eye of a microscope, often returning to wriggle infinitely magnified before the dreamer's eye. But those things were known, safely contained behind glass, and lifeless. What I saw on the long-ago afternoon had come from the wild, and still lived. It was the color of a particularly unpleasant death, and, to this day, I do not know precisely what it was.

Of those to whom I have spoken of the monster, few can agree as to its exact identity. Most assume, as I did and do, that it was a parasite, one even providing a lengthy Latin name that almost immediately escaped my mind. Another suggested that the chipmunk may have been pregnant, and what I saw was an ejected fetus struggling to survive with its body as yet incapable of doing so independently. The latter is unlikely. Chipmunks give birth in reasonably large numbers, not to single offspring. The offspring of most rodents are born hairless, but most come into the world colored a warm, living pink, not the slimy black of the monster.

Whatever the identity of the monster, I destroyed two lives with one .22 pellet that afternoon. If the parasite theory is correct, I probably brought mercy to the chipmunk, ending a life that could only have been tormented by the interloper wriggling and feeding within it. If the monster was indeed a fetus, then somehow I feel twice guilty. Which is odd, for I have never felt any remorse for the lives of the other five chipmunks I killed that afternoon.

Perhaps it is better that the monster remain nameless, and, therefore, remain a monster to me. It was and is a true reminder of the true significance of what I was doing that hot July day. In my innocence, I veritably skipped about with the old air gun, grateful for the temporary escape from boredom and the promised small reward. But, as I entertained myself, I gave no thought to the fact that I brought death into the sunlit pasture, a pointless, unnatural death that should not have been dispensed so casually. Perhaps it was just as well that my hand, however, innocently motivated, brought the monster into the light of that summer day. For I would never forget again.

ℰℴ   ℭℛ

Blooming Where Planted

I had been walking too fast, a mistake. In-depth nature observation requires subtlety, and subtlety is the first casualty of motion, especially hurried motion. In some environments, one tenth of one's accustomed pace can be too fast, and one hundred yards ought properly be an afternoon's journey. A forest with rich soil during a summer of abundant rain is definitely among them.

I walked a trail following a former road and, on reaching its end, set off into trackless forest. But I did not slow my steps to match the pace the terrain deserved. Oak blurred into ash into maple into basswood, and wildflower blurred into weed into grass. The roadside world smears into featurelessness beyond the window of a moving car, and nearly all of the earth's surface is lost from the height and speed of an airliner. The natural world, or at least the details holding its greatest wonders, blurs to anyone refusing to experience it at its own speed.

Variations in surroundings, however, will reveal themselves even when haste and inattention have obscured everything else. A roadside sunflower grabs the eye even at freeway speeds, and no aircraft can fly fast enough to erase a rainbow. Some maverick features invariably insist on being noticed.

It was one such anomaly that caught my eye that afternoon, an anomaly in the sense that it was situated far from its proper place. Far from road and former road, I came upon an apple tree, one of great age by the diameter of its trunk. A commercially grown tree would long since have ceased to bear and been sawed down to make room for a successor. But these limbs, though scarred and twisted by countless winters, were heavy with fruit.

This was, I assumed, a "wild" apple, the product of some

long-ago bird that had dropped a seed upon receptive soil. Or perhaps the hands that had planted it were human after all. Nearby, in other seasons, I have found lilacs and clumps of day lilies, possibly the landscaping efforts of some long-ago settler whose homestead had long since gone to ground. The yard, once graced by lilacs and lilies, might well have held an apple tree as well.

The abundant fruit on the tree posed a mystery of sorts. For, though an isolated apple tree can and will bear some fruit, such a heavy crop suggested that this one had been pollinated by another apple tree. Pollen had been carried to the gnarled old apple tree's blossoms, in all likelihood, by a common honeybee, one of the most reliable apple pollinators.

Honeybees have been known to fly as far as five miles in search of nectar if no closer source is at hand, though half a mile is more common in promising locales. Within half a mile of the "wild" apple tree, therefore, in all likelihood could be found both another apple tree and a colony of bees, either civilized in a neat white hive or living the wild life in the hollow trunk of another tree.

I knew of neither an apple tree nor a beehive in the neighborhood, though it was impossible, of course, to know every detail of every yard and pasture within a radius of half a mile. The bees knew and the heavily-fruited tree I had encountered knew.

No one would pick the ripe apples that autumn. What promised to be a bountiful harvest would go to waste, at best becoming food for deer and chipmunks. But the tree lived and bore fruit. That was enough.

80   CR

The Curtain Across the World

Rain had fallen the previous evening, dropping half an inch of moisture onto ground already saturated by earlier storms. The rain ended as the sun set, fading gray to black behind a screen of heavy cloud. With the coming of night came a drop in temperature. Even the wind seemed to have grown tired of blowing across the sodden landscape. Somewhere far away, it rested.

The cool, silent atmosphere drew some of the moisture from the ground and into the air, to hang suspended, hovering precisely at the dewpoint. What had fallen from the clouds became a cloud again, a low, rolling cloud spread across the surface of the earth to smooth away all detail and clarity behind a screen of milkiness known best by the simple name that carries all the ominousness of night and the silence of the deepest shadow: fog.

A row of trees borders the gravel driveway that leads to my home, passing roughly one hundred feet from the house and ending at the two-car garage approximately the same distance away. At gray sunrise, trees, driveway, and garage were all invisible from the house. The landscape was wrapped in the sort of fog that is a staple of mystery and romance novelists, the bane of mariners and motorists, that closes airports and robs every other traveler of confidence.

Perhaps the most basic of human fears is that of the unknown. Fog forces the unknown closer than usual, pushes the familiar farther away. Visibility within the fog bank was perhaps fifty feet, and, though I knew what lay beyond was the familiar surroundings of my yard, there was fear out there as well. Silent fear. Lurking just out of sight in the silent landscape.

Few greater temptations exist, however, than that of any curtain hiding some unknown from view. Rare is the person confronted by such a temptation who will not attempt at least a clandestine peek at the hidden unknown, even if he or she must abandon certainty to see what waits behind the curtain. When the curtain obscured not merely an object but an entire landscape, I could not resist. I dressed for the dampness and headed out into the fog.

The air was so sodden it seemed incapable of carrying sound. My footsteps on damp, glistening grass were nearly silent. With easch step came a little thrill at the top of my spine, a sensation of small discovery, perhaps a fear of what might be out there to be discovered. Nevertheless, I walked on into the curtain that had been drawn across the world, seeking to draw it aside or at least get a glimpse beyond it.

A lake lies five hundred feet below the house. I set my feet upon the path that led to the shore. Moisture loves moisture, and I was certain that the fog would be most dramatic at the water's edge. A few steps and the house was lost to sight. My world had been reduced to a few feet of path before and behind me, lined by trees on either side. Beyond that, the curtain was drawn tight.

At the shore, the curtain pulled closer still. Not until I approached within twenty-five feet of the beach could I see it clearly. The water was stilled to mirror perfection. But it reflected only featureless fog.

My old friend, a former rental canoe now nearly half a century old, waited on the shore, its bow pointed out into the hidden water. The curtain beckoned, and I followed. I stepped into the canoe and pushed it out into the lake.

I drifted for some time, letting the momentum of my initial shove carry my lightweight craft across the motionless water. The shoreline vanished almost at once. Vague shadows seemed to hover just beyond the curtain that drew tight around me. The silhouettes of trees, perhaps, but attempts to focus on them proved fruitless. As I drifted farther into the lake, even the shadows vanished, leaving me alone with the fog.

On reflection, I realize that there was an element of foolishness to what I did. The lake is roughly half a mile wide at the point where I took to the water. With neither landmarks nor compass to provide any sense of direction, I could conceivably have drifted for some time before finding any shore, to say nothing of the finding the one from which I had departed. While I could not see what lay out there in the fog, I could be almost certain that it contained no other travelers. The ripples from my canoe spread across a perfectly stilled surface. Any other traffic would have sent ripples of its own to tell me that another was out there somewhere. I was quite alone, and none knew my whereabouts. The situation was not overtly hazardous, but, nonetheless, those who seek to confront nature on its own terms are generally best advised to leave a detailed itinerary in case of accident.

But I thought of none of these things. The curtain that had been drawn across the world had become my world now, for it had hidden every recognizable object save the canoe. I drifted, and, as the canoe slowed to a stop, I dipped my paddle gently into the water. The blade shattered the surface's mirror into a thousand ripples that rushed outward and vanished behind the curtain.

The human senses, when deprived of stimulation, seek all the harder for it. Eyes strain in dim light, ears focus intently in silence. A sleeper's hand, thrust desperately into the air and out of a dream, seeks the comforting firmament of the wall.

As I paddled onward into the fog, my eyes and ears strained for some hint of what might lie ahead. But there was, seemingly, nothing to be seen or heard. Once, only once, a distant dog barked. The sound was quickly swallowed in silence. The dog might have been a few yards away, or a few miles. There was no way to tell. Fog may carry the sound of a train whistle from ten miles away but muffle a nearby voice.

I paddled on, oblivious to the clammy air, the chill beginning to make its way through clothing dampened by the touch of the fog, oblivious to the silence of the morning and the fear that, in retrospect, dogged every inch of my way. I saw only the curtain and sought only to see what might lie behind it.

Quite suddenly, I saw indistinct shadows ahead, the

counterparts of those I had left behind as the canoe had glided out onto the lake. I had made my way to the other shore, and trees were struggling from the fog to warn me of its nearness. I had come as far as I could in search of what lay behind the curtain, only to find that it was not far enough. I sat in the canoe and began to realize how far I had come from home and what a difficult passage I would have to get back to the shore I had left.

Now the fear I had first sensed before leaving the house was rising, becoming impossible to ignore. I did not dare to turn the canoe around, could not face the necessity of paddling back into the curtain, which, I now realized, lay just as much behind me as before me. Some intangible answer to the all-too-tangible questions posed by the fog might well lie somewhere in its sodden folds. But it was an answer I no longer wished to find.

I would not have to. The still air had hovered almost precisely at the dewpoint all morning. Now it had cooled infinitesimally. The air could no longer carry its burden of moisture. It began to rain.

Now, at least, there was sound—low, monotonous sound to be sure, but reassuring sound nonetheless, the whispering of the curtain as it was drawn aside. In seconds, the circle of visibility around me began to widen. Shoreline shadows became recongizable silhouettes, then trees. The rain fell and washed the curtain away. And when, sodden and shivering, I looked over my shoulder, I saw that my own shoreline was visible once again. Return to the world I knew would now be easy.

I pointed the canoe out into the lake, dipping the paddle firmly now for speed and out of the knowledge that the surface was no longer a fragile mirror, dappled as it was by countless raindrops. Halfway across, I began to laugh, and the rain laughed back at me. We had seen behind the curtain, the rain and I. I by attempting to force my way through it, the rain by lifting it. But, though our means and quite possibly motives varied considerably, we shared laughter born of the relief of knowing that there was no longer any need to look.

                                              ℰᎧ   ᏨᎡ

Under the Umbrella

In Minnesota, a sky of fresh, puffy cumulus clouds means summer. It can also mean rain, as I once discovered to great surprise and eventual delight.

The sky was not on my mind that afternoon. A blue sky dotted with clouds is among the more innocuous of summer sights, one quickly superceded by the hope that led me into the forest that afternoon. The hope that somewhere on a stump or fallen log, I might find a sulphur shelf mushroom or "chicken of the woods," among the most delectable of edible fungi.

Half a mile of ambling along a trail through old pasture and long-undisturbed forest had brought no results. Though I looked high and low, I found no sign of the unmistakable white, yellow, and orange tiers of the sulfur shelf. But I searched so intently that I did not notice the approach of a cloud bank larger, darker, and nearer the ground than those that had passed before. Only in recollection did I notice that the sound of the breeze had changed, deepened by the approach of falling water. But when a raindrop splashed on my shoulder, I took the hint.

If I hurried, I might be able to reach my car in ten minutes. But the rain was very close; it would not allow me that much time. If I tried to run for it, I would end up getting soaked, hardly a disaster but far from fun. As another raindrop struck me, I began to look for a place to wait out the shower. Tentative sunlight already appeared in the western sky beyond the cloud bank; I would not need to hole up for long. I had seen no lightning, nor heard either thunder or the freight-train roar of wind that meant a serious storm. The approaching storm cell held no danger, I concluded, only inconvenience.

A few yards away, the trail led from open, airy pasture into shadowed forest. A massive red oak stood at the forest's edge, its gnarled and sprawling limbs heavy with abundant leaves completely obscuring the sky above. The ground beneath the oak, unlike that in the open area before it, remained dry even as the pasture began to glisten with moisture. The oak's trunk was at least eighteen inches in diameter. The tree had withstood countless seasons and storms; it would provide a haven from the shower.

The rain began in earnest as I hurried to the base of the ancient oak. The temperature dropped, and I pressed close to the coarse, deeply furrowed bark, half-hoping to find warmth there. The trunk, alas, was no warmer than the forest shadows but, at least, provided shelter from the wind. The dense canopy of leaves above me shuddered and murmured under the touch of the rain, and a few stray drops made it through. But I remained reasonably dry even as my surroundings quickly became sodden.

Around me, a curtain of grey had been drawn beyond the forest's edge. It permitted no sound but the whisper of a million tiny splashes multiplied by each other, no movement but that of leaves bowing beneath the weight of drop after drop. But then, from the corner or my eye, a stirring . . . .

It was a cottontail rabbit. Young, perhaps half its eventual adult size. Its fur was matted with moisture, and there was a labored quality to its hopping, as if it were fatigued by the rain or at least resigned to being caught out in it.

Perhaps fifty feet from the oak beneath which I had found shelter, another mature oak stood. The ground beneath it was as dry as that beneath my own improvised umbrella. The rabbit hopped to the base of the other oak, and there, very close to the trunk, it stopped and turned to face me.

I will not say the rabbit looked at me, for it gave no real sign that it was aware of my presence. But it turned toward me, and its dark eyes, like those of every rabbit, held a constant expression variously interpreted as fear and innocence. Its gaze seemed to fix on my own. Something passed between us, I'm sure. Something that made both of us stand quite still and remain very quiet.

And that was how we waited in the rain. It was a wait of only a few minutes. But they were precious minutes. Given the choice, I would have asked for more.

The sound of afternoon breeze began to rise once again above the patter of falling rain. The sun flickered to the west; then I had a more hopeful glimpse of it, and finally a golden glow warmed the old pasture and illuminated every spent raindrop as the shower passed on to the east. Without haste or effort, and almost without sound, the cottontail turned and hopped away. Water still dripped from every branch, but the rabbit sensed what I suspected. The rain was over.

The forest had provided not only an umbrella but a companion with whom to share it. For the first time in my life, I was glad to have been caught out in the rain.

℘   ℭ

The Forest for the Trees

Within sight of the room in which I write, in a narrow strip of mixed forest between a former three-acre field planted with apple trees and the gravel road serving this area, a tall and ancient white oak tree stands. An average specimen of a mature white oak, perhaps sixty feet tall, the tree widens from frail and continually flexing twigs at its crown to a base easily exceeding a yard in diameter. The white oak grows slowly and for a long time. Individual specimens have been known to live in excess of eight hundred years. While this one does not begin to approach such a dramatic age, it has almost certainly kept its vigil beside the present-day site of my home since the time of the Civil War.

To lumberjacks, the white oak is prized for its wood, among the most valuable hardwoods found on the North American continent. A scientist might consider it worthy to mention that a mature white oak absorbs sufficient exhaled carbon dioxide and emits sufficient oxygen to meet the respiratory needs of several human beings. A historian might muse that locked in the heart of the oak beside my home may be wood grown from a breath absorbed by century-old leaves after being exhaled by Abraham Lincoln. To the romantic, the oak is whispers in the spring breeze, shade on sunny days, a shelter from storm and simultaneously a target for lightning. But, like the elephant touched by seven blind men who stood at its feet and believed it to be seven different things—all incorrect—the oak transcends definition. It holds a meaning, a strength all its own that stretches far beyond any name or description applied to it by any discipline of the heart or mind.

The oak about which I write has endured winter, summer, sun, and storm. It has thus far escaped the lightning, though some unknown force a number of years ago killed two limbs protruding from the trunk about fifteen feet from the ground. The oak does not seem troubled by their loss; it has limbs aplenty, and when one is so old and so massive, perhaps the loss of a couple of minor appendages is unworthy of notice.

One of the dead limbs fell a few years ago, revealing a small hollow behind the point at which it once joined the trunk. A pileated woodpecker promptly enlarged the hollow and raised a brood in it one year. The tree did not seem to mind at all. Fresh scratches around the opening to the hollow this past winter indicate that another tree-dweller, possibly a squirrel, found a home there more recently.

The second dead limb still clings to the tree. This past winter saw the bark peeled from it and scattered on the snow beneath it. Insects moved into the dead wood, insects that served as meals for the woodpecker or nuthatch that patiently pecked away at the peeling bark. Stripped of its protective covering, the dead limb has faded bone-white. It will rot and fall in a relatively short time, especially on a human scale. In terms of a tree that has already survived two complete human lifetimes, the time needed to slough off the limb is hardly any time at all.

The fallen limb may reveal another hollow, which may in turn provide shelter for some other creature. It may also provide entrance to the insects that fed on the dead limb or to their

brethren, which might eventually lay waste to the entire tree and bring it down at last. In my brief acquaintance with the tree, I have seen it survive drought and flood, frost and blistering heat without complaint or any outward sign of suffering. But something will bring it down eventually. Sooner, recent developments would indicate, rather than later.

At the base of the oak is a rough-sawn wooden stake festooned with a bright plastic ribbon. It is a survey stake, placed by the county highway department as a preliminary to a major road improvement project scheduled to begin within the next few months. The road will be upgraded, the ditches deepened and widened. The new ditch on the north side of the road will reach its deepest depth at a point coinciding with the location of the white oak.

The roots of the patient oak are deep and strong. But they will not survive the onslaught of a bulldozer. The road crew will succeed where the seasons could not. Only a fool would question the need for roads and their maintenance. Only a fool would place a tree above the needs of a community. I find it worth noting that, while any fool can pluck a flower or cut a tree, no one, however wise, can manufacture one.

കൗ ൧൩

Rain, Sand, and Shattered Wings

Rain fell the night before, the sort of quiet, steady rain without storm that lulls one easily to sleep. Morning found the grass washed and brightened, the trees seemingly eager to reach up for the sunlight.

An area of open ground newly washed by rain is a fine place to look if one is searching for new things. Fresh earth after a rain is a slate wiped clean, ready for a new tale to be written upon it. As I walked to the mailbox that morning after the rain, I followed the trails left by earthworms summoned from their burrows by the rainfall. Here and there a straggler still worked his way along the gravel driveway, leaving behind a gracefully twisted track. Why earthworms never travel in straight lines is a mystery to me. Perhaps it is their way of finding food or the result of dodging obstacles invisible on a human scale but gigantic to the worm. Perhaps the reason is pure pleasure, much as a skater, given the space and freedom, tends naturally to fall into arcs and circles.

Halfway down the driveway, I spotted a patch of intense color, the vibrant black-striped yellow of a tiger swallowtail butterfly, its wings spread wide. I moved toward it slowly, careful not to let my shadow fall upon it, in the hope of getting a close look. But after a few steps, I realized my caution was unnecessary. The lovely wings lay twisted and limp, and a large part of one had been torn away. The swallowtail was dead, perhaps fallen from the radiator of a passing car. It had fallen earlier that morning, undoubtedly, otherwise the rain of the night before would have washed the color from the fragile wings and beaten them into the ground.

Though obviously dead, the butterfly was moving, inching along the ground with an odd, hesitant motion. My initial shock at the discovery gave way almost at once to curiosity. Clearly, something was happening that could not be seen or appreciated from a human height. I lay down on the moist gravel, hoping for a glimpse of the source of the movement.

Beneath the stilled wings of the swallowtail, several ants were hard at work. Each had taken hold of part of the butterfly,

and, working as a team, the ants were shifting it toward their nest. A small ant hill stood at the driveway's edge a few feet away; perhaps it was the intended destination.

I was fascinated to see the tiny creatures working in congress, to be granted such a clear demonstration of their incredible strength. Were humans possessed of proportionate strength, an infant could easily lift a fair-sized car. It may seem little enough for half a dozen ants to move the corpse of a butterfly, but when one stops to consider that each of the butterfly's legs was longer than any of the ants involved, the scale of the feat becomes somewhat more apparent.

A number of other ants milled about the small hill that I took to be the home of the returning foragers. When the swallowtail got within range, they would swarm over its body, tearing it into pieces small enough to be carried down the winding tunnels of their nest, there to be stored until needed as food. The swallowtail would live again, becoming part of innumerable ants.

Several hours later, I returned to the spot. I found the ant hill at once but no trace of the dead butterfly. Either I had been mistaken, and it had been dragged to some other nest, or the eager ants I had seen milling about the hill earlier had already completed the task of dismembering their find and carrying it below.

I have wondered since what happened to the brilliant yellow and black wings that retained such beauty even when stilled and faded by death. Were they, too, cut into manageable pieces and lugged down into the ants' nest? Might the wings of a butterfly be excellent food for an ant? Or could it be that in some chamber below that tiny hill of sand, a few black-and-yellow scales have been placed to catch faint rays of the sun that reach down through the narrow entrance? I'd like to think so.

℘   ℭ

The Question of the Spider

A photograph is a moment. It may be a moment of personal triumph or of national tragedy, depending on the photographer and the subject. Or a photograph may be a moment that, when recalled, serves only as the birthplace of a question.

From the brilliant green surface of the floating bog mat rose four stems from which dangled nodding flowers of a deep rosy hue. Beneath the flowers, tightly curled leaves formed the deceptively beautiful insect traps of pitcher plants. Twenty feet of open water lay between the edge of the bog and the nearest solid shoreline. The nearest pitcher plant was a similar distance inside the edge of the bog.

The inaccessible holds an irresistible attraction to nature observers, particularly those who carry cameras into the wilderness. With the aid of my brother and an aluminum canoe, I set out to approach within camera range of the pitcher plants, a feat involving stepping onto the living surface of the bog.

A floating bog is, for the most part, a dense mat of tangled moss, grasses, and roots. Beneath its bright green surface lies water or liquid mud, mud rendered highly fertile and highly acidic by generations of plant matter grown, died, and rotted. Small trees—spruce, cedars, and tamarack—grow in bog mats, giving the surface a deceptive appearance of strength and solidity. This deception can and has caused such places to be lethal traps, for the trees do not stand on solid ground, and the organic soup beneath the bog mat can be twenty or more feet deep. One false step can reveal just how fragile the mat actually is. While it may not be strong enough to hold up a person, it can be more than strong enough to hold a person down. Scandinavian and Irish bogs have yielded corpses, mummified by acidic mud, of those who fell or were pushed into them more than ten thousand years ago.

As my brother steered the canoe to the mat's edge, my main thought centered on photography. But I was thinking, too, about how drowning in the darkness under the bog would be a particularly horrible way to die.

The bow of the canoe slid easily onto the edge of the mat. Fifty feet away, a small black spruce wobbled slightly as the ripples of our arrival passed through the fragile firmament. The pitcher plant I sought was perhaps five feet away. Taking a deep breath, I stepped onto the surface of the bog. It took my weight, yielding only slightly.

Holding onto the canoe for support, I laid a paddle on the "ground" to spread my weight somewhat in the manner of a snowshoe. With camera held high, so it would be the last thing to get wet should I start to break through (cameras and water definitely do not mix!), I inched toward the cluster of plants I hoped to photograph. The distant spruce wobbled a little more, but my footing held.

Since a bog mat consists entirely of alive and dead vegetation, I was not terribly surprised to discover that I was not the only living creature prowling the bog that day. My companion, however, was unlikely to be troubled by the possibility of breaking through the mat. As I began focusing my camera on the pitcher plant, still balancing precariously on my canoe paddle "bog shoe," I noticed a small black spider sitting on one of the delicately cupped leaves of the plant.

The spider held still while I photographed the pitcher plant from several angles, including a close-up of the leaf upon which it sat. Moments later I worked my way back to the safety of the canoe. As I regained my seat, I thought little of the spider, feeling only relief at not becoming a potential find for future archaeologists.

Not until the photos I had taken were processed did the question posed by the photograph of the spider arise.

The bog mat lacks several nutrients that pitcher plants require for their survival. They, and several other bog plants, acquire these nutrients by capturing insects. Within each "pitcher" is a pool of rainwater, to which insects are attracted by an irresistible scent secreted by the plant. But having once entered the cupped leaves, the unfortunate insects find escape nearly impossible. Downward-pointing hairs lead them toward the waiting pool to be drowned and digested. The leaves of the pitcher plants often become choked with the indigestible exoskeletons of drowned insects.

The spider I saw while thinking only of my own safety was crawling up the leaf of the pitcher plant, possibly attracted by the scent rising from the deadly pool within. I had been drawn to the bog by the pitcher plant as well. But the plant that had forced me to tread carefully so as to avoid being trapped by the bog was only a curiosity to be observed and captured on film. To the spider, too small to be concerned by the fragility of the bog mat, the plant was a serious hazard. Size poses a paradoxical advantage in the world: the large are freed of countless matters of concern only to the small, but exposed to countless other risks that the small may never notice.

Did the spider, a few minutes after my departure, fall into that tiny pool, becoming food for the cupped leaves and the nodding, rosy flowers? Or did it only pass unharmed across the plant on its way to another, safer destination, much as I did myself? I'll never know, but, to this day, I cannot look at the photograph without wondering.

෪   ෬

A Falling Star

Perhaps human beings first domesticated fire in an effort to stave off the inevitability of night. Fear of darkness is among the most basic of human impulses. Many children believe, as do a surprising number of adults, that something lurks in the dark, something to be avoided.

To an observer with the courage to defy this age-old fear, however, the outdoor night is filled with wonders with irresistible appeal. The patient stars, the lonely eye of the moon, the shimmering veil of the aurora borealis, the sounds and occasional shadowy glimpses of animals never seen by daylight—all combine to draw me, at least, out of the house during the wee hours at all times of the year.

Had I never ventured outdoors by night, I would never have heard the fluttering leap, the "flight," of a flying squirrel, nor seen the frenzied circling of a bat in the full moon's light, or learned that billions of mosquitoes hovering in the treetops actually produce a sound of surprising volume. And I certainly would not have seen the star fall.

Following a day during which the mercury had passed the ninety-degree mark before noon, I was walking along a narrow gravel road. The still midnight air retained the day's thick lifelessness. The sky was clear and moonless; the grass shimmered beneath a heavy dew.

On similar nights, I have spent hours lying on my back in the middle of fields, adjusting my gaze until nothing earthly intruded and I could imagine myself falling upward into an endless sea of stars. But that night I walked, without destination but certainly not without purpose. The stillness of the night held anticipation, as if something remarkable were about to happen. And, quite suddenly, something did.

To the north, an impossibly large object streaked brilliant white across the sky. It yellowed, faded and shrank dramatically as it approached the horizon, until, when it vanished below the tree line, it was only a tiny red ember. The event required far less time than will the reading of its description. My estimate was that perhaps two seconds elapsed; in all likelihood, it was actually less. Had I been looking in the wrong direction or blinked at the wrong moment, I would have missed it entirely.

Tumbling blindly through space, a large mass of stone or iron, perhaps even a derelict satellite or rocket booster, had met the upper reaches of the atmosphere. Friction produced by its speed had heated the mass to incandescence, burning most of it away as it streaked across the sky, slowing as it plunged through increasingly dense air toward the earth. The object, which first tore glowing across the northern sky, might have weighed a ton. What actually struck the ground, as the red ember undoubtedly did a millisecond after I lost sight of it, was probably no more than fist-sized.

Major meteor showers can be seen during eight months of the year. Mid-August marks the return of the Perseids, among the most dramatic of such events, At its peak, August 11 through 13, an observer might catch sight of as many as one hundred "shooting stars" per hour. Most, little larger than dust specks, quickly flare and vanish, their visible life barely sufficient to register on the eye. Meteors of sufficient size to reach the ground are few and far between, coming singly and observed only rarely.

Those are the simple facts of the matter, the realm of science. I prefer to think of my experience somewhat less coldly, recalling a momentary pang of sadness at the idea that a star had fallen from the heavens and a still-lingering frustration at the knowledge that I would never know where it had landed. I have long wished to hold in my hand something that had come from outer space. We are space travelers ourselves, after all, on a journey that has lasted billions of years and which may have neither destination nor ending. But without an occasional reminder, it is all too easy to forget.

On that muggy night, I had my reminder. And a reminder, too, that there is indeed something in the dark. Something which, to this day, I continue to seek on a regular basis.

ଔ   ଷ

Two Chance Encounters

No certainty exists in observing nature. Days of searching the most inaccessible area might turn up nothing of interest. But, on other occasions, unexpected wonders literally fall from the sky in the most ordinary locations.

I had been lugging the camera through the woods all morning and most of the afternoon and, with shoulders aching from the weight of my equipment, was on my way home. It was late summer. Leaves and roadside grasses had lost their spring shades, fading to a dull green that seemed old and weary of life. When a tiny patch of brilliant green practically screaming of vitality appeared on the road ahead of me, it caught my attention at once. When it also became apparent that the object moved under its own power, I determined to see what it was.

 It was a caterpillar nearly the size of my thumb, brilliant green and nearly translucent, with vertical brownish streaks at intervals along its body and a few fragile protruding hairs. A caterpillar of one of our larger forest moths, the fragile ghosts of summer generally flying unseen and lit only by the moon.

But which moth? I could not be certain without checking, and proper identification required the caterpillar. Left on the road, it would probably be crushed under somebody's radials anyway, so there was little reason to worry about disturbing it. I allowed it to creep onto my hand (cautiously, for several large caterpillars carry poisonous spines that can cause a painful rash), carried it to the car, and set it on the passenger-side seat, where it passed the journey to my home in apparent comfort.

A field guide revealed the caterpillar to be the larval stage of a polyphemus moth, named after the Cyclops slain by Jason's Argonauts because of the eye-like spots decorating its wings. A relatively common species among Minnesota's larger moths but still a rarity. The idea of keeping the caterpillar in a jar and possibly pupating it into the moth occurred to me, but the likelihood of its survival all the way through metamorphosis should I do so was slight. The best course, I decided, was to return the caterpillar to the forest.

Basswood leaves are among the preferred foods of the polyphemus caterpillar, according to the field guide, and a basswood tree stood at the edge of the yard. I held the caterpillar near a low-lying branch. It seemed reluctant to leave my warm hand, but finally gripped the twig with its tiny feet and shuffled onto it segment by segment.

Though I had had my fill of photography for the day, it seemed a shame to leave such an unusual find unphotographed. I got the camera and tripod, returned to find the caterpillar waiting on the branch. The lighting was just right, the air almost perfectly still.

As I watched and photographed, the caterpillar began to crawl along the twig, probably in search of shade or a leaf to defoliate. Watching through the lens, I followed it as it went, clicking the shutter every so often as it offered an interesting pose.

So absorbed was I in watching the caterpillar that I barely noticed when something tiny dropped from above, landing on the camera. A leaf or twig, I assumed. Until I raised my eye from the viewfinder and got a good look.

Perched atop the camera and seemingly looking straight at me was a northern walkingstick, one of the true oddities of the insect world. Able to move only slowly and possessing no defensive abilities to protect it from predators, the walkingstick evolved into a shape that mimics a twig to an uncanny degree. The specimen on my camera was a male, judging by its brown color. The female of the species is the bright, fresh green of a newly sprouting branch.

I lifted the walkingstick from the camera and set it on a convenient basswood leaf. Forgetting the caterpillar for the moment, I turned the lens on the new discovery, getting sever-

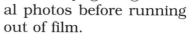

al photos before running out of film.

Another idea came to me: what if I could get the caterpillar and the walkingstick in one picture? Would they move sufficiently close together if I waited and watched? First, I needed a fresh roll of film.

I found the film and quickly returned. But both of the day's finds had apparently made other plans; they had wandered off. Neither the caterpillar nor the walkingstick was anywhere to be seen. Though wonders can drop into one's life at any time, they do so in their own time, and often they depart as quickly as they come. Sometimes the best picture is the one that got away.

                                                   ℰ   ℩℺

The Old Government Road

Perhaps two hundred yards east of my home winds a narrow road. Originally blazed through the wilderness during the 1850s, the Old Government Road, as it is known to the locals, became obsolete almost overnight when a rail line, following essentially the same route, was completed a few miles to the west in 1870. Quickly abandoned, most of the road has been forgotten. Some distance to the south, several miles have been kept in reasonable repair and remain in use by local travelers. But the vast majority of the original 185 miles, including the stretch passing east of my home, have not known traffic since the days of the horse-drawn stagecoach.

Just beyond the gravel road that now serves my immediate neighborhood, a forty-acre field straddles the former thoroughfare. Planted in corn, soybeans, or alfalfa in alternating years, the field has long since been plowed free of any trace of the old roadbed. About a mile to the north, a sign marks the spot where the Government Road once ran through what is now a heavily forested area. But a century of probing roots and levelling frosts have filled the ditches and smoothed the crown. No trace of what the sign commemorates remains.

On the south side of the field east of my home, a fragment of the road clings to a sort of existence that, thus far, has defied the dual efforts of man and nature to obliterate all but its memory. Here, a broad gully bottomed by swamp passes between to fields. A rushing river just after snow melt, a stinking swamp filled with frogs by mid-summer, the gully also holds a small memory of the Old Government Road.

What remains of the road enters the gully from the north through a cut in the bank, an excavation made both to lessen the grade and possibly to provide fill below, where the road crossed the swamp. Rain has washed through the cut again and again, turning it into the beginnings of a tributary gully that, should the farmer ever stop plowing his field, will probably eat its way across that now nearly-level expanse. But so long as the field is maintained, the plow will restore whatever the rain carries away.

Decades of rain have washed away any resemblance the cut may have borne to part of a road. It is a gully now, no more. Only the brown-eyed Susans, wild strawberries, and occasional wild roses, plants that thrive on poor, disturbed soil, give the slightest hint that human hands once touched this place, heaping and smoothing clay and gravel over topsoil.

Descending into the gully, one passes through several layers of growth. Fence row plants form the uppermost layer; goldenrod, clover, and burdock thrive on the abundant sunlight and fertilizer from the edges of the field. Then come the grasses and disturbed-ground plants—hillside weeds, small shrubs, and tree seedlings that have only recently begun to find a footing there. Finally, near the bottom of the gully and on either side of the swamp is a narrow strip of fertile soil and occasional shade, which supports a few more delicate plants. Hepaticas and violets in spring, oxalis ("sauerkraut" to those familiar with the acidic tang of its leaves and stems) later on. But these grow in a select area bounded on one side by the sloping bank of the gully and on the other by the waterlogged swamp at its very bottom. Beyond the margin drawn vaguely by rising and falling water, only willows, cattails, and several varieties of stout, sharp-edged grasses grow.

But at the bottom of the gully, one can at last find some recognizable trace of the Old Government Road. Here the road could not simply follow the contour of the land. Load after load of soil, some of it probably carried down from the cut by which the road enters the gully, was hauled into the swamp and dumped, then topped with a firm layer of sand and gravel after the level of the roadway had been raised above that of the spring floods. This brief, perhaps hundred-foot-long stretch of former roadway, by the combination of its relatively intense intrusion upon the landscape and the fact that it passes through an area unsuitable for exploitation, remains in a sense intact.

From the cut in the northern bank of the gully, looking south, one can clearly see the raised and rounded contour of the roadbed extending through the swamp, eventually reaching the far side where its distinctive shape flows up the remains of another cut in the southern bank, vanishing perhaps halfway up the slope. In the absence of any traffic, the surrounding vegetation has done its best to cover the old thing. But the mixed sand and gravel of the former roadbed offer little in the way of nutrients. A sparse covering of often sickly grass, along with a few tiny flowers of indeterminate species and a few wild strawberries that have crept down from above are the best that has come along so far. With close scrutiny and some imagination, the remnants of ruts left by narrow steel wheels can still be made out along the crumbling crown. Perhaps the grass, sparse as it is, has helped to keep the ruts from washing entirely away.

The flood following every snow melt has done its best to wash the road away, with some success. Whatever culvert may have once existed to guide water underneath the roadway has long since collapsed, and the seasonal stream has made its own way, breaching the old roadbed in two places. Within my memory, it was possible to cross the swamp by way of the road without getting wet feet. But the breaches have widened and are no longer jumpable. The road remains for the moment, but the water is winning. In a relatively short time, it will reclaim the gully for itself.

Barely the width of the narrowest modern-day road, the Old Government Road was once the only reliable route between what would become the metropolitan areas of Duluth and the Twin Cities. Countless travelers passed this way; stagecoaches and wagons with mail and supplies of every variety, loggers bound for the great pine stands of the north, immigrants seeking their way into a new land, and troops bound for the Civil War.

But now the road has been forgotten; even the ground it crosses is doing its best to forget. Within a few years, the willows and swamp grasses will close over the last bit that hides in the gully east of my home, just as the late Cretaceous ferns closed over the last of the dinosaurs. During one visit to the place several years ago, I found a large bone protuding from a part of the roadbed recently washed over by the spring flood. A relic of some long-ago beast of burden? I cannot say. But I will wonder for a long time.

The gully will remember the road for some time yet, perhaps long after I am gone. But in time, it will forget, as the earth in time will forget us after we have gone. The grass and the disturbed-ground flowers will be only too happy to grow over our roads and cities, given the chance. Some flowers only grow on scorched earth; others sprout with pleasure from the cracks of crumbling ruins.

I have been to the gully and to the hundred-foot stretch of vanishing road many times. It is a haunted place to me, a spot where I can never escape the knowledge of how far away my ancestors are, of how far the human race has come since their day and, to some extent, how little we have changed in the intervening century. Easily I stand upon the long, low, crumbling mound, the remains of the roadbed; with some effort and imagination, I detect a trace of an echo of hoofbeats and narrow wooden stagecoach wheels. But it is difficult for me to convince myself that what I hear is only the wind through the tall grasses of the swamp.

℘   ℭ

The White-Fronted Goose

In the time of year when the world seemed to be sleepily holding its breath for autumn, the geese came to the ditch below my grandfather's house. Spring greens had faded to dull summer hues; here and there an impatient leaf had already fallen. The air still held warmth, but shortening days and cool nights spoke eloquently of the winter waiting to take its first bow. I was a boy then, but even now I remember the geese well.

We were a family of city dwellers in those days, making our way to the country on weekends for a few breaths of unsmogged air, a few evenings undisturbed by the howl of sirens, a few nights' rest in rooms where shades did not need to be drawn against the glare of streetlights. My grandfather owned a 120-acre farm, though in the year the geese came, he had retired from farming. His fields and forests were the site of many wonders to a boy just discovering the natural world. The ditch—actually a narrow stretch of water connected to a lake—had always been one of the most fascinating spots on the property, teeming with insects, tadpoles, and, on occasion, fish. When we arrived at the farm one Friday evening, my grandfather said that three geese had taken up residence in the ditch.

The next day, my father and I crept to a spot near the shore of the ditch. From a hiding place behind a conveniently situated woodpile, we watched the geese for over half an hour.

Two of the geese were instantly familiar as "Canadian honkers." The third was a dusky brown species I had never seen before. A white-fronted goose, my father told me.

During the half hour we watched them, the geese swam together as one, a flock in miniature, gliding nearly silently across the surface of the ditch. Taking care to remain unseen, we managed to avoid disturbing them. When we had seen enough, we sneaked away, leaving the geese swimming in silent formation just as we had found them.

My father explained that the white-fronted goose had probably lost its mate. Geese mated for life, he said and, having lost the chosen partner, will not seek another. But neither will they remain alone. Generally, a "widowed" goose follows the first geese it encounters after its loss, becoming part of that flock. In the case of the white-fronted goose, it had found companionship with a mated pair of a different species.

When we visited my grandfather's farm a week later, the geese were gone. They just moved on one day, he said; they do that at this time of year. But Canada and white-fronted geese do not follow identical migratory schedules, nor do they always winter in the same part of the world. Assuming that the white-fronted goose followed the Canadas when they left, it fought down one of its most basic instincts in doing so.

I have often wondered what the Canada geese thought of the white-fronted goose. Was it accepted as an addition to their "flock"? Or was it an intruder, a clinging, unwelcomed nuisance? Could it have even seemed a rival, a threat to the relationship of the mated pair? Do geese feel such things? I do not know. But, recalling the white-fronted goose, I know they feel loneliness. I often wonder what happened to that unfortunate bird and how things turned out, whether the tale of deep sadness somehow turned out to have a happy ending.

Much has been said and done in the name of loneliness. Countless human lives have been shaped by the desire to escape it. But who among us, I wonder, has known the loneliness of the white-fronted goose? Who has been forced by circumstance and instinct into a life alienated not merely from friends and family, but from species?

The autumn months will bring the sounds of geese to many ears across the north as they begin their long flight to warmer climes. Many times I've heard their mournful calls passing overhead, sometimes late at night, when it seemed as if only I and the geese were awake in a still, silent world. Often I have welcomed their calling as a sign that the season is turning and that change is in the air. But often, too, I wonder if I have heard only a casual announcement that geese were en

route, or the desperate cry of a solitary bird, an unanswered plea for a companion, for something to acknowledge a reason for and meaning to its existence. And at such times, I wish I could do or say something to ease the agony I hear.

80 ∞ 03

One Tiny Fall

I had been wandering through the same forested area for six straight afternoons, shoulders aching under the weight of camera bag and tripod, seeking a particular arrangement of maple leaves. In so doing, I was violating a rule every nature observer should obey without question: I was looking for something specific, rather than keeping my eyes and mind open to whatever might come my way.

Seeking a specific object or species in nature is almost a guarantee of not finding it. Any number of other wonders can be missed along the way. Scan the ground too closely for mushrooms, and one might never see the eagle gliding overhead. Turn to gaze up after birds and, chances are, a booted foot will land in the middle of a nice patch of wildflowers.

Too, I had decided on the composition I wanted to photograph long before beginning my search for it. A cluster of maple leaves, arranged just so and beginning to shade red or orange as their tree readied itself for its long winter rest. I could see the leaves clearly in my mind's eye, but attempting to impose one's inner vision on the unrestrained natural world is also a bad idea. Nature photography can be compared to taking a picture frame into the woods in search of something to put inside it. But the choice of what will wind up inside that frame cannot, by necessity, be entirely the photographer's own. Nature provides its own choices and tends to frown on those who would choose for it.

Perhaps because of these two minor crimes against nature, I had searched for six days without success. The seventh day was an almost perfect day for photography, clear and with very little wind. As I entered the forest a little after noon, my hopes were high.

My wishes seemed likely to be rewarded. In only a few minutes I found what I wanted. A small clearing set in the middle of dense forest revealed at its edge a single maple branch bearing a vague resemblance to a frail and withered arm. At the end of the branch was a cluster of leaves still bright with summer's green but delicately tinged with orange, red, and purple as the coming autumn touched and revealed the sugar that ran with sap through their veins. The leaves were arranged almost precisely like the composition I wanted. And they were centered in a rare shaft of forest sunlight. But I would have to hurry. In a few minutes, the sun would move, and the leaves would be hidden in shadow once again.

I set up the tripod, chose the appropriate lens, and prepared to take the picture. In moments, the leaves were centered in the viewfinder, the lens focused, and the exposure set. I cocked the shutter and held my breath, waiting for the leaves just to stop nodding in the faint breeze.

Quite suddenly, the leaves were still. My thumb tightened on the cable release. And, with the faintest of whispers, the largest and most colorful of the leaves released its hold on the twig that had supported it through the entire summer, and tumbled softly to the ground.

I stood with my mouth open for some

time, staring at the empty space that had ruined my carefully compsed picture. Anger and more than a few bad words filled the clearing, but I knew it was useless. The picture was gone. After a long time, I put the camera away. Frustration gave way to laughter and finally to wonderment. But not for some time.

Why did the leaf choose that moment to fall? It was still quite green, still, to all appearances, filled with life. One might have expected it to remain on the tree for at least a couple more weeks. But perhaps it was impatient and did not want to wait any more. Perhaps it was shy and did not wish to be photographed. More likely the warmth and movement of my breath, or even the stirring of my shadow through the warming sunlight, were sufficient to break the leaf's attachment to the tree, an attachment weakened by time and due to end. Leaves, I must remind myself, possess neither reason nor emotion.

I never photographed the cluster of leaves I sought that week. After the lesson of that afternoon, I opened my eyes to what the forest wanted to show me and was rewarded several times over. But what will remain longest in my mind from that interlude is remembrance of my singular experience of the leaf that could not wait.

"The Autocrat of Russia," wrote Mark Twain, "possesses more power than any other man in the earth, but he cannot stop a sneeze." Human beings can move mountains, alter the course of rivers, smother countless acres under pavement. But there is no human effort or desire that can prevent the fall of a single leaf.

℘   ℘

Bittersweet Thoughts

Several days of rain during the previous week had stripped nearly every leaf from every tree. Frost had singed the grass a dull brown, leaving only occasional traces of the color of summer. Heavy overcast held the sky; its greyness reflected from the water perhaps one hundred yards from the country road I walked. Only the wind seemed alive.

In the ditches and the fringes of the surrounding forest, every late-fruiting plant carried a bumper crop on its stems. In late October, most such "fruit" consists of burrs and other annoyances that find their way onto clothing, leading to lengthy removal sessions at home. Having endured several such sessions in recent days, I was content to stay on the road.

Ten days would bring the opening of the deer-hunting season. The forest would come alive with eager, rifle-bearing hunters clad in blaze orange. Not being terribly comfortable either in such clothing or with the idea of accidentally finding my way into someone's rifle sights, the first two weeks of November generally find me indoors. Thoughts that this afternoon walk through a rather depressing landscape might be one of the last for a while were with me constantly.

In the ditch ahead, a tiny flash of brilliant orange caught my eye; the flash on first impression seemed too intense to be natural. A bit of litter, I thought, or perhaps a flag left by the telephone company to mark the location of buried cable. Few things in nature have anything to gain by being easily noticed. Consequently, few adopt colors that lead to such notice.

But there are exceptions, one of which I had just discovered. I approached the spot of color that had caught my eye, and it proved to be part of a large clump of bittersweet. Bittersweet is a curious climbing plant that favors open, sunny areas in which to spread its twining, vine-like branches. Here, among tall dead grass and barren stems of prickly ash, it had thrived to an extent I had never seen before.

A single cluster of bittersweet berries had first attracted my notice. At closer range, hundreds of similar clusters were easily visible. In the wake of recent frosts, the nearly fluorescent orange summer hulls of the berries had burst, peeling back like petals to reveal the brilliant red fruit within.

Bittersweet berries are somewhat unusual in that they retain their color when dried. They are, therefore, prized by amateur and professional florists for use in dried arrangements. Consequently, a thicket of bittersweet is in jeopardy any time it grows near a populated area. While I have encountered it many times, most of the stands I have seen consisted of only

a single plant bearing a few clusters of berries. Finding a patch sprawled nearly one hundred feet was unusual, and its location beside a well-traveled road made its undisturbed existence even more unexpected. I could only conclude that either no one had noticed it or no one cared to. Or perhaps both.

Although bittersweet is, in a sense, put at risk by its brilliantly colored berries, likewise that coloring is responsible for its survival. The orange husks and brilliant red berries are immediately apparent to the eyes of birds, which feed upon them readily. The seed contained in the berries is indigestible, capable of passing through a bird without harm either to the bird or itself. And the uncounted millions of bittersweet seeds that make that unscathed digestive journey end up scattered across the countryside, where, if they fall upon favorable soil, they grow into new twining branches that call out for attention with still more bright berries.

As I stood among the bittersweet, I thought of the hunters who would soon venture into the forest dressed in the brightest shades technology can produce in search of a quarry that wears the colors of the forest. Both adapt their coloration for the same reason: a desire for self-preservation. It is curious that hunter and hunted should use opposite means of attempting the same end.

It is curious, too, that what can insure safety for a human in the forest should also be responsible for the survival of an otherwise unremarkable plant. That in a world filled with predators and hazards, sometimes being noticed is the best way to stay alive.

℘   ☙

The Icing on the Cake

The school bus rattled past the end of the driveway at 9:30 A.M., struggling along much slower than usual. It headed away from town, and that could only mean one thing at that hour: school had let out early for some reason. In this case, the reason was obvious.

The preceding day had brought long hours of steady rain falling in temperatures hovering at freezing onto ground that had been frozen solid for two weeks. We had had no snow as of yet. A quarter inch of rain became gleaming ice covering everything. That morning, the weather forecast had been for heavy snow. At ten A.M., the sky had still not brightened sufficiently for the neighbor's yard light to shut off. Without doubt a storm was on the way. Snow on top of clear ice would render roads all but impassable. The children had been sent home from school early to insure that they would not be stranded by the weather.

"The calm before the storm," most commonly employed in summer, usually is associated with the sudden violence of a thunderstorm. The calm before a snowstorm is often of considerably greater length. Since dawn there had been no wind.

The bare tree branches in the front yard bent under the weight of the encasing ice. Only the row of pines along the driveway remained relatively ice-free. The oils keeping needles alive and unfrozen through the winter seemed to protect them from all but the heaviest frosts. But in the still, moist morning air, though free of ice, the pine boughs were frozen in space as completely as the burdened branches of the other trees.

A clump of tall grass stood near the edge of the garden. Formerly an uninteresting mass of lifeless brown, every blade had come alive anew, thickened and brightened by jewel-perfect ice. In sunlight, the grass would have gleamed. But with the temperature hovering a mere degree below freezing, a few minutes of sun would have melted the ice, freeing the dead grass of its finery and laying it away to sleep unnoticed once again.

My uncertain footing reminded me constantly that I tread on ice on the edge of melting. Within the confines of the yard, I was able to find sufficient traction on the grass. But on the unbroken surface of the driveway, skating rink conditions prevailed. Every so often, cars struggled by on the road. Those not spinning their tires or wobbling as one wheel after another lost its traction were making less than fifteen miles per hour.

I set out for the lake below the house. Between the house and the lake is a hill perhaps one hundred feet long and sufficiently steep to speed one's heart and breath when it is climbed quickly. As I picked my way along the path down the slope, I wondered if I would be able to find sufficient traction to climb back up. My boots preceded me twice, and, both times, I was able to stop only by braking with the seat of my jeans. On other such occasions, I have carried a walking stick with a sharp tip capable of penetrating ice. That day, I had left it behind but wished for it with every sliding step down the hill.

My progress was slow, but patience and several more falls finally brought me to the lake's edge. Looking south, I saw the storm and, with it, approaching winter—deep gray sky, deeper still the water reflecting it. In everything, a heavy stillness. At the shoreline, a thin rim of ice formed. I shivered and turned back to face the hill.

Successfully climbing the hill remained uncertain for a time. I made the last part of the uphill journey on hands and knees, and, when I arrived at the summit and proudly rose to my feet, the ice decided to have the last word and threw me flat on my face. I heeded the warning and headed indoors.

The snow began a few hours later, big sloppy flakes that melted quickly. But, as night settled in, they began to stick. Sitting in a comfortable chair with a cup of cocoa that night, watching the TV reel off an endless series of accident reports, I was glad I hadn't tried to go anywhere that day. But glad, too, that I had gone out.

☙   ❧

The Ghost of Autumn

While walking on water, I came upon a ghost.

A week of clear nights and still days had seen temperatures falling well below average and considerably below freezing. Though the ground remained snowless, the lake lay hidden beneath a glossy sheet of ice extending from shore to shore. The evening of the seventh day of the cold snap found a breeze rising from the northwest and clouds on the horizon, hints of an approaching storm. The time seemed right for a walk.

At the water's edge, dead grass and low-hanging branches stood encased in frozen spray from the final waves to break upon the shore before the lake had frozen. Riffles left by those waves on a strip of sandy shoreline had frozen solid, remaining as reminders that water had once splashed there.

Near shore the ice had thickened perhaps two inches, a marginal depth for safe support of a person's weight. Undoubtedly, it was thinner farther out, a deceptive and potentially deadly trap. Not wishing to tempt fate, I resolved to remain above water no deeper than the height of my boots.

The ice creaked, bending slightly beneath my weight as I stepped onto it. At the shoreline, the edge of the ice shifted ominously, threatening to give way. But it held, and I moved carefully across it, past the crystal-embedded grass and the frozen-riffled beach.

Among northern hardwoods, the red oak seems most reluctant to release its leaves at summer's end. Many retain crowns of rustling brown throughout the winter, dropping them only when the new crop of leaves arrives. Ahead of me, a low-hanging limb of just such an oak extended over the lake. On the ice beneath the limb lay about a dozen leaves that had decided not to wait any longer.

I had pulled my cap tightly around my ears in a largely vain attempt to keep the rising wind at bay. Yet the fallen leaves neither fluttered nor drifted away across the polished ice, when one would expect them to do both. I wondered why.

A moment's examination at closer range revealed the secret. The leaves had fallen during the previous night, while the air was still, remaining on the ice during the equally windless day. Absorbing the sun's warmth, each leaf had melted a small pool of water beneath itself, a pool which, with the coming of evening, had quickly frozen. Each fallen leaf was frozen firmly to the surface of the ice.

I grasped at a stem and tugged. The leaf resisted at first, then came away, leaving behind a few brown flakes. And an unexpected wonder.

As the water beneath the leaf had frozen, it had formed a perfect impression of the leaf. Every vein, every ripple in the skin of the fallen leaf was flawlessly recorded in white frostwork reminiscent of a design etched in glass. But no artist's hand could have produced such detail. What lay before me was nothing less than the ghost of autumn, haunting the shadows beneath the oak branch.

The molded impression of the leaf was a white of almost unimaginable brilliance. But as I watched, the delicate tracery began to reflect a hint of palest rose. The sun was setting; the wind still rose. I thought of my fragile footing and the cold water below. Shivering, I turned away from the fallen leaves and the spirit of the previous season that lay with them.

With every step, the ice protested my weight. Reaching the shoreline with dry boots seemed almost a miracle.

A few days later, heavy snow blanketed the ground and the ice, burying the ghosts that haunted its polished surface. The oak tree continued to drop a few leaves from time to time, but these were quickly lost in snow or carried away by wind. Under the snow, the lake ice froze deep and hard. Before the winter was over, I would venture onto it many times. But it was not the same.

In a few months, people will marvel at the reawakening of life and speak of the "miracle of spring." Few will stop to consider that spring will also melt the lake ice, and no one will be able to walk on water anymore.

80   03

The Voice of the North Wind

No sound seems quite so lonely as the voice of the north wind in winter. Rushing endlessly over barren landscapes, driving before it snow, which in turn drives every living thing into hiding, it carries in its every movement and every breath a hollow pleading against its unwelcome solitude. It is the voice of the full moon on a still night, of a freight train passing beyond the fringes of a small and darkened town, coming from somewhere very far away and bound for an even more distant place. It is a voice all have heard but few have ever tried to answer.

The call had begun in the darkest hour of the night, whistling around the edges of the storm windows, grasping at the shutters, finding one loose and banging it against the house. Awakened, I lay listening in the darkness, hearing the

wind's words but grasping the meaning of only one: snow. Autumn had fallen, winter awakened, and the north wind had brought it near.

In daylight hours, I would certainly have gone out to investigate, to stir the first drifting flakes of winter with my hands, to melt a few on the tip of my tongue. But it was too late, and I was too tired. The wind that shook the house only rocked me to sleep.

I expected to find the wind and the storm it had brought gone upon awakening. But, ignored, the north wind had grown angry, and the howl to which I had dozed paled beside that to which I awakened. An urgency in that desperate cry demanded that I look out the window. When I did, I looked into the face of the sort of storm countless grandparents recount to grandchildren, who listen politely but do not believe.

By midmorning, a local television station called it the Megastorm. Before it was over, nearly thirty inches of fresh snow blanketed a landscape that had retained distinct traces of green only twenty-four hours before. Meteorological records of every sort fell with the passing hours, and most of the state closed down for the duration. Tightly closed houses became oases of warmth in a wind-whipped desert of white. It was a day for huddling close to fires, for reading postponed books and accomplishing long overdue bits of tedium. It was no day for travel; that first glance from the window convinced me to postpone my small plans for the day.

It was my intent to remain indoors. But, as I went about the morning rituals of dressing, coffee, and breakfast, the voice of the north wind was with me always. Seemingly louder at every instant, it seemed offended at my ignoring it during the previous night. Still, I could not understand its words, but the desperation in its voice transcended language. Several times I turned toward it, the better to hear.

Winter is the season of memories, and when the season comes hard and fast, the memories too often follow suit. I had, for the most part, only my own company to keep that day; a host of recollections sought to relieve my solitude, succeeding only in placing it in sharp and agonizing relief. I was alone with the north wind when so many were not, among them several who had long since abandoned my company but whose painful memory, it seemed, would remain with me forever.

Through the morning, the north wind called to me. It moaned of loss and of longing and of searching endlessly for things it knew it would never find. All the dark of the previous night filled its voice, as well as all the cold of the snow that wrapped the earth. But, another coldness lurked there as well, the chill that grew only in an empty heart. I was alone, annoyed at the disruption in my schedule, already growing tired with the effort of struggling to force down unwanted memories. Halfway through the afternoon, I found myself alternately exhausted and enraged.

Perhaps it was only a combination of boredom and whimsy. Perhaps my mind, starved for occupation, merely responded to what was most readily available. Or perhaps the voice of the north wind truly did call out to the usually-submerged primal element in every human heart. But quite suddenly, it seemed I understood the words whispered by the voice of the north wind. Somehow, I felt that it, in turn, might understand the cry I longed so desperately to give voice. But I knew I could not do so from within the house.

My winter clothing was still packed away, need for it not having been anticipated for several weeks. It was a matter of some effort to unearth a full complement of snow boots, gloves, balaclava, scarf, and parka from the confusion of the closet. But I found and donned them all and made my way outside.

The wind waited. It snatched the screen door from my hand, threatening to tear it from its hinges before I regained my grip on it and latched it tightly. Snow had accumulated in the yard to a level nearly even from the front porch; my first step beyond its confines was lost knee-deep in fluffy cold. A few steps through it were exhausting.

The north wind seemed to laugh. Strength born of anger at its mockery drove me onward, step after straining step. It was a ten-minute struggle to the end of the driveway, a distance of perhaps two hundred feet. I hoped to find the road plowed, an open area on which to wander while I argued with the wind that threw snow in my face and laughed in my ears even as they echoed its receding loneliness.

But the storm had kept even the snow plows in their lairs. A few desperate or foolhardy travelers had forced their vehicles through the snow, leaving wheel tracks, which had already partly refilled. The road was easier walking than the pristine snow of the driveway, though not much. I walked north. I looked into the face of the wind. I wanted to call out, to utter howling, desperate words that would be lost in the roar that whipped its own loneliness around me. But my tongue held no syllable so eloquent as those that forced themselves into my ears.

In retrospect, what I did was dangerous. With little visibility, an approaching car, however unlikely, would be upon me before I could see it, its motor noise lost in the merciless wind. And that same wind stole heat from my body at a relentless pace. An ankle twisted in an otherwise trivial fall could have made me the nucleus of a snowdrift at any time. But I walked and looked straight ahead. In the snow, I could see little or nothing; I do not know what I may have been looking for. But I walked. I listened. I tried to speak, to free the pain born of solitude and unforgiving memory. But I had not the words. I could only listen and be called onward by the one that did.

The wind had lured me out; the wind eventually brought me to my senses. My footing was uncertain on the slick surface, my vision blurred by snow. An especially strong gust, an invisible hand seemingly drawn back all the way to the North Pole and violently released, reached down and shoved. It grasped at my bulky clothing, spread it wide in a credible substitute for a sail. And I fell.

Into a snowbank, fortunately, and without twisting, spraining, or damaging anything other than my dignity. I sat up, paused for a long moment, not considering that my improvised seat was in the middle of a public thoroughfare. I was awed, startled, and, suddenly, a little frightened.

The wind, having pushed me away, seemingly rejecting my company, had changed. It had swung a bit to the west, and there was no longer mocking laughter in its voice. Beneath the ever-present loneliness and desperation, I heard a new note suggesting that, though I had not spoken, I had perhaps been heard and understood. I had been given a warning, in the only language the wind could speak, that my surroundings were not fit for anything warm and alive, that it was time for me to make my way indoors.

I was cold, and the fall had brought home the foolishness of my errand. The wind seemed to calm a little as I got to my feet and turned my back on it. It had nearly erased the trail I had made during my walk, but I retraced my footsteps as well as I could. And, as I did, I tried to convince myself that what trickled down my cheeks was only the remnants of a few melting snowflakes.

Coffee remained in the pot, a warmth so intensely welcomed after the razor's edge of the storm that entering the house was like walking into an embrace. I threw my snow-encrusted clothing in a pile, filled a mug and went into the living room. A picture window faced north, and I stood at it for a long time, gazing out at the swirling snow and hearing, as in the night before, as in the awakening hours of dawn, as in the desperate minutes of my foolish walk, the voice of the north wind. I raised an opened hand, pressed it to the glass. A greeting, perhaps, an attempt to offer touch and reassurance to one who, by nature, could do nothing but run from it. The wind had come a long way and had far to go. And I wished it well.

൧ ൭

The Fire Dragon in the Snow

A two-day blizzard arriving early in the cooling season of the year blanketed Minnesota with snow in record-breaking proportions. One week later, though travel had become fairly routine once again, a trip of any distance remained a luxury.

The second weekend in November saw the opening of deer-hunting season. Though I carried no gun, the early snow called me into the forest. On Sunday, I donned the required blaze-orange and set out for a favorite wilderness spot.

Cold had followed the storm. The snow remained deep, refusing to melt or compact more than slightly. Walking was made doubly difficult by the fact that, beneath the snow, the ground remained unfrozen. Between snow and earth was a layer of slippery, boot-grasping slush.

Deer had broken a trail into the aspen forest I sought to wander. But when traveling one hundred yards through the snow required at least three times as much time as walking across open ground, I realized I could not go farther. I marvelled at that deer's could make their way on thin, fragile legs.

I was cold, wet with snow melted on my trouser legs. Fatigue borne of disappointment slowed my footsteps as I turned back toward the road.

I saw a movement on the trail, a tiny movement, but nonetheless surprising in a forest seemingly empty of all life. On first glance, it appeared to be an insect. But insects were gone for the season.

Three inches long, glossy black like wet leather, and dotted with tiny bluish-white markings, a blue-spotted salamander moved slowly yet desperately down the trail. A denizen of summer, quite out of place in deep snow, the amphibian should have been hibernating. The falling temperatures typically preceding heavy snow by some weeks should have sent the salamander into an inactive state, waiting beneath leaves, logs, and finally, snow, for the return of spring.

The early snow had indirectly brought the normally reclusive creature into plain sight. The blizzard that had wrapped the earth in deep white had come before the onset of extended cold weather. The salamander found itself buried above ground too warm to allow it to hibernate. It had probably muddled about beneath the snow since the storm until, possibly given a passage to the surface by my footprints, it made its way into the light.

Salamanders were once nicknamed "fire dragons," the name originating from their habit of wintering inside hollow logs, to emerge when the logs were placed on a fire. An old myth would have one believe that, like the legendary phoenix, salamanders were born in flames.

They are, however, more comfortable in ice than in fire. Salamanders possess the unique ability to freeze solid and revive on thawing without ill effect, a talent studied at great length, though research has never yielded a complete explanation. But this salamander was struggling; if it froze on top of the snow, a scavenger would find it long before spring. Its movements were slowing toward a final halt as I watched.

I picked it up. Warmed by my touch, the salamander's struggles quickened but then stilled as if it sensed it had found a haven. My backpack held a thermos of coffee. I place the salamander in its stainless steel cup, where it rode in seeming contentment during the walk back to the road and the drive home, almost without stirring.

A woodpile stands beside my house, but it has been untouched since the stove was removed after a chimney fire several years ago. Its shelter would provide protection from the snow and moisture to keep the salamander's skin damp and glossy. Perhaps the salamander would find sufficient insects to feed it until the ground temperature dropped enough to let it sleep for the remainder of the winter.

I dug through drifted snow until I found a corner of the tarp covering the woodpile. Beneath it, a frost-rimed hollow led into the shadows. I set the salamander on the ground before it. It hesitated at first. Then, moving faster than it had since I had first set eyes on it, it crawled into the darkness. I put the tarp back in place, weighting it with a scoopful of snow to insure that the haven would not be violated by the wind.

Many people had gone into the forest that day in hopes of taking an animal's life, and some, presumably, succeeded. My own brief journey led me to save a life. I had thought the day wasted, since I had been forced to turn back so soon. But the fire dragon in the snow had shown me otherwise.

ℰℴ   ℭℛ

The Shadow with a Shadow

A bird feeder in winter is a community of sorts, a crossection of the surrounding area. It is a community that tends to become more closely knit as the season wears on, burying or exhausting the few natural sources of food left over from warm months.

It is also a community that exists by the rules of a definite hierarchy. The smaller birds—goldfinches faded to olive drab for winter, chickadees, snow buntings—seem to rest near the bottom. They dare to approach the feeder only when no larger bird is in sight and often content themselves with searching the snow beneath the feeder for whatever their superiors have dropped. The grosbeaks seem to have a firmer claim on the feeder itself but flee at the approach of a bluejay. The bluejays, like all who lie beneath them in this particular order, flush at the first glance of one of the large woodpeckers.

The snow beneath the feeder is also the domain of a number of gray and fox squirrels, who burrow tirelessly for sunflower seeds or bits of cracked corn overlooked by the finches. The search must be profitable more often than not, for it is not uncommon to see half a dozen or more squirrels working their way around the feeder.

By and large the squirrels take little notice of each other, though each maintains an invisible perimeter that, if crossed, renders the offender liable to be chased immediately up the nearest tree. As the winter passes, the circles shift and grow, widening dramatically around the males, in particular, as spring awakens old territorial and biological imperatives. By the last snowmelt, one is unlikely to see more than one squirrel under the feeder at a time.

Midway through a winter that had begun with nearly

three feet of snow in a single twenty-four-hour period, a new resident entered the tiny society under my backyard bird feeder. In retrospect, I had noticed the newcomer some time before realizing what it was. During a morning interlude over coffee in front of the picture window facing the feeder, I had seen a hint of dark motion beside a fallen log on the fringes of the yard. Its source proved to be invisible. Only a shadow, I thought. Perhaps a reluctant leaf still clinging to a twig and fluttering in the breeze.

That afternoon, I saw the shadow again. This time it stood in full sunlight, perched ten feet above the ground in the cleft of a small tree. A familiar shape of unfamiliar color: ebony marked by faint highlights where sunlight caught at soft fur, particularly that which abundantly covered its long, distinctive tail.

It was a melanistic or "black" gray squirrel, a rare variant hidden within the genes of the most familiar member of the species. The past summer, it seemed, had brought the genetic jester into the light. The squirrel was young in appearance, somewhat smaller than its fellows and lacking much of the abundant store of fat with which squirrels hold back the northern winter. It did not appear to have eaten well in some time.

As I watched, the black squirrel eased down the tree in which it had perched and moved toward the space beneath the bird feeder, where half a dozen squirrels of more common appearance were picking through the snow. Against the sun-lit snow, the squirrel seemed darker than ever. The shadow it cast was light by comparison. I watched, fascinated and hoping it would approach closely enough for better observation. Melanistic squirrels are not as rare as albinos, of which I had seen several. But I had never seen a dark squirrel before.

In fact, I never got a close look at the squirrel. As soon as it approached within ten feet of the bird feeder, one of the feeding squirrels launched itself at the intruder, driving it back to its perch in the tree. There it waited for some time, until the feeding activity in the snow had returned to normal. But another attempt to descend and approach brought another attack, this time from a different squirrel. The process continued during the entire part of the afternoon that I sat and watched.

The black squirrel must have been terribly hungry, for it never stopped trying to approach the feeder. Its persistence was difficult to understand, but even more difficult to understand was the other squirrels' refusal to tolerate its presence. It may have seemed a competitor, to be sure, but, by the same token, so would each of the others who fed peacefully in the same area. And a food source sufficient for six would undoubtedly have fed seven as well.

The shadow with a shadow remained nearby for several days. Once or twice, I saw it burrowing beneath the bird feeder but only when no other squirrels were present. When the black squirrel fed, no birds seemed willing to approach.

One day it stopped coming. Perhaps it simply grew tired of fighting with the other squirrels and moved on in search of a place to live without being bothered. Perhaps it vanished into the stomach of an eagle, a coyote, or a neighbor's cat. Jet black fur would make its presence obvious in snow or even against the bark of a tree, where an ordinary gray squirrel would be relatively inconspicuous.

In this fact, perhaps, is the answer to the question posed by the hostility of the other squirrels. Perhaps they feared the black squirrel's visibility would bring death down on all of them. Perhaps they were only reacting, as most wild creatures will, to the presence of nonconformity. In a world defined largely by the roles of predator and prey, the security of the herd is perhaps the oldest and most widespread. Nearly all species possess at least some tendency toward it.

At least, I hope that's all that I saw during those cold winter days. The events haunted me through the long nights of the season and remain with me still. Perhaps we are not the only species susceptible to the disease of prejudice. Perhaps the hunger in the black squirrel's belly was the consequence of another emptiness—one in the hearts of the other squirrels.

I hope not.

෨   ഌ

On the Track

Fresh-fallen snow is a blank page, a tablet upon which tales are often written. The story inscribed on the fresh white surface may be comedy or tragedy. Or, on occasion, mystery.

Eighteen inches of fluffy snow had fallen on the night before. The world basked in the fresh light that can only come from the fresh-scrubbed sky following a winter storm. A light of unparalleled brilliance etched the finest detail of every twig and grass blade upon my eyes with incredible clarity.

The snowplow had cleared the road to the river reasonably well. Another day would elapse before the roadway was widened to its usual dimensions, but there was room for me to park next to the bridge. Fast-moving sections of river steamed in the near-zero chill. Slower water long-since covered with a skin of ice lay smothered in mounded white.

I tried to walk down the steep bank, finally gave up and slid down on my bottom, stopping with a feet-first plunge into a snowbank. When I stood, I was waist-deep in soft snow. Fortunately, the snow thinned rapidly nearer the water's edge.

I had thought myself the first living creature to be out after the storm. The snow through which I struggled was wind-polished and untouched by any sign of an earlier visitor. But, as I approached a small mound near the water's edge, I saw that something curious had occurred there not long before.

From one side of the mound a hole perhaps six inches in diameter indicated that something had recently emerged from a burrow. The unknown creature had plowed through the snow for several feet, leaving a furrow of similar proportions to the hole from which the trail began, then spun about in an abrupt circle. At one side of the circle sketched in the snow, the imprint of two large wing tips was visible.

My first thought was that the track had been left by a grouse emerging from its nighttime snow cave. The furrow, I theorized, had resulted from the bird's attempts to lift itself high enough above the soft snow to be able to flap its wings properly and thus gain the air. A fine theory, but one which was almost immediately proven wrong.

On closer examination, the trail had been made by a creature leaving the tracks of four feet at the bottom of the furrow, between which ran a fine line, which could only have been sketched by a dragging tail. Hardly the signature of a grouse.

The river, providing year-round access to open water and, therefore, to the waterfowl and fish—the staple diets of many raptors—is a common winter hangout for hawks and eagles. As I studied the track, I realized that not one, but two animals were responsible for the story written in the snow.

Earlier that day, some small animal, probably a muskrat, had emerged from its burrow and ventured forth in search of food. Its fat body plowed through the snow, leaving a trail decorated with its footprints and the drag marks of its tail.

Only a few feet from the burrow entrance, however, a sudden threat appeared above. The shadow of descending wings, the silent but sensed approach that could only mean death. The muskrat, or whatever, began to turn around, seeking a quick return to its haven. But the soft snow hindered the animal already awkward on land. Just as it completed its turn, the predator reached the ground, leaving the tracing of its wing tips to mark its landing.

The final chapter to the story, the eventual fate of the unknown creature, was not written in the snow. No trace of blood or fur, no sign that a hawk or eagle had killed and eaten nearby. So it may well be that as I contemplated that strange trail in the snow, its creator watched from just inside the entrance to its burrow. Quite possibly thinking, as countless other creators have before it, that writing a story, whether one's medium is a sheet of paper or the surface of fresh snow, is no easy task.

80   CB

The Stream of Life

There were mallards in the river that year, a flock of nearly one hundred that had been fooled by the flowing, open water until cold blocked their migration south and stranded them for the winter. The water, it seemed, was warmer than the air, for the ducks emerged from it only on occasion and for brief periods. Day in and day out, they swam in the icy current, occasionally ducking under the surface in search of whatever food might be found, at other times rising as a flock toward the nearby town to scavenge the leavings of the feed mill.

Mallards are highly adaptable birds, able to thrive, or at least tolerate, city or country, summer or winter, provided that open water is available. Nonetheless, I felt sorry for the stranded ducks as they faced temperatures that kept me indoors more

often than I liked. The only possible fuel for the inner fire warming a body is food, and food was unlikely to be available in abundance around the river in winter. I purchased a large sack of cracked corn and began taking a pail of the stuff to the river's edge each day.

The mallards seemed to welcome the attention, rewarding my efforts by approaching closer with every visit. Within a month, the sound of my car approaching was sufficient to bring the flock noisily to the shore. And on more than one occasion, some of the mallards fearlessly pecked corn from the palm of my gloved hand.

Among the stranded flock was a hen that did not swim as the others did. Her head was turned sharply to one side as she swam, as if it pained her to hold it straight. An injury, I assumed. The life of a wild duck is not easy, and surviiving a Minnesota winter is difficult indeed. There are many things with which to collide, and most of them have sharp edges.

The injured hen was among the more timid members of the flock, so it was some days before I discovered the exact nature of her trouble. But one day she emerged from the river to peck at the corn I had tossed near the water's edge, and, as she did, I got a clear look at the side of her head that had always been turned away from me. It was a smooth expanse of skin and feathers, lacking only one feature. The mallard had no right eye. Whether it was the result of injury or a caprice of genetics, I cannot say.

The mallard's odd pose while swimming had been adopted as a means of turning its single eye forward. I was reminded of the periscope of a submarine; a single unblinking lens trained carefully upon its chosen object. I wonder often if the one-eyed mallard could see more clearly because it had to look with greater care and precision than one better equipped for sight.

After my discovery, I made a point of looking for the one-eyed mallard during each of my visits to the river's edge. When I saw her, I tried to make sure she got some of the corn I brought. For, if I felt sorry for the stranded mallards in general, I felt doubly sorry for the one facing winter with only one eye.

One day, the one-eyed mallard was not there anymore. At first, I thought I had simply overlooked her. There were nearly one hundred ducks in the flock, and one mallard looks much like another. Succeeding visits brought no sight of my favorite, however. In time, I came to realize that she was gone.

Among the seasonal inhabitants of the area near the river were several eagles, ruthless predators for whom a mallard would have made a fine meal. Especially in the hungry month of January. And especially a mallard unable to notice the silent swoop of a raptor's wings if it approached from the hen's blind side.

I never found any trace that my feathered acquaintance had met such an unhappy end. I only know that I never saw her again. When warmth returned to the area, the stranded flock broke up and spread throughout the countryside.

When I think back to that winter and the time I spent on the banks of the river, I think of those mallards persevering and surviving in the face of the worst the season could throw at them. Most of all, I think of the duck with the single eye, forever looking forward, and perhaps in the end losing her struggle with the world because she could not look backwards at the same time.

℘   ℭ

The Grouse, the Glass, and the Gourmet

The January afternoon had been stilled by the intense chill that came only after a heavy snowstorm. The sun brought light but no warmth; it glared from every surface with an unnatural clarity uncomfortable even through dark glasses.

The storm had left far too much snow on the driveway to ignore, though the cold made doing so attractive. Starting the snowblower was an hour-long chore, and clearing the driveway required an hour more. A strong wind blew straight down the driveway, and no chill is quite as piercingly intense as that carried by a faceful of wind-driven January snow.

A ruffed grouse had been busying itself along the margins of the yard as my father and I worked. In the silence after the snowblower had been put away, with the only work remaining the shifting of a few shovelsful from in front of the garage door, came a sudden explosion of wings as the grouse lifted into a pine tree. There it sat, feathers fluffed against the cold, nipping at the fresh buds at the tip of the branch. The bird seemed to take little notice of us, and, as the exertion of removing the final traces of snow began to take hold, we took little notice of it. The afternoon was growing long, and the fact that the job was nearly finished seemed to make the snow all the heavier.

Quite suddenly, a loud thud came from the direction of the house, a sound amplified by its unexpectedness. A snowstorm wraps the world in silence; one's ears become somewhat lax when surrounded by a freshly smothered landscape, and sudden sound stuns them all the more. I turned toward the sound just in time to see a shadow drop into the snow in front of the living room window. My first impression was of a spent snowball falling away from the window, but there was no possible thrower in sight.

107

"What was that?" my father asked. I could only shake my head even as I moved to discover what had happened.

It required only a few moments and some imagination to reconstruct the events leading to the sudden sound. The pristine snow before the picture window was marred by a crater slightly larger than my fist, the sort of trace a mischievously tossed snowball might indeed have left. But what it marked instead was the final landing place of the grouse, which, having flown directly into the living room window, had ricocheted from the glass and fallen into the snow to lie with a broken neck.

I picked up the dead bird and held it in an outstretched hand, slightly shaken at finding it still warm but utterly without life. Seeing it, and realizing what had happened, my father came over for a look. It was an occasion that called for some words of regret, however perfunctory. A proud and wild creature had come up against the barriers civilization is prone to erect. As is the common result, it had perished.

My first thought was to remove some tail feathers and keep them as a sort of memento. As for the bird itself, I planned to throw it into the woods, leaving the scavengers (in all likelihood, the neighborhood dogs) to make use of it.

The idea of eating the grouse came a little while later, as my father and I talked and I held the still-warm body in my hand. It had been in good health; we had seen it eating. And we knew it had died recently; in many respects, it would be far better fare than a bird felled by a shotgun, for there would be no tooth-threatening pellets embedded in its flesh.

I found a knife, and together we skinned the grouse. Steam rose from it, and I remember that, strangely, I no longer felt cold. In the bird's gullet were the brown pine buds it had been eating, and they looked disconcertingly like worms.

He was a tough old bird, taking hours to roast in a covered Corningware dish before the tiny drumsticks browned and the flesh of the breast fell away from the bone. Even well done, the meat was dry by comparison with force-fed domestic fowl; stringy and strong-flavored, as one might expect of the flesh of a creature that had dined on the buds of a resinous pine. But I ate every bite, and it was delicious.

∓… •∞

A Call in the Night

The night was cloudless and sufficiently cold to stiffen the nylon shell of my jacket. Across the northern sky, clouds of charged particles riding the wind of the sun struck the upper atmosphere, glowing in shifting auroral splendor as streamers of blue, green, and occasionally red. It seemed odd that such a dramatic display should be utterly silent.

I walked a field covered by a foot of snow crusted heavily by several days of warm weather that had melted nearly half of what three months of winter had deposited there. The ice crust held just enough of my weight to deceive, then gave way beneath each step with a strident crunch. Walking was difficult, the pace set by the field, with each step lifted high to clear the snow and then falling low as it broke through the crust again.

Night walks are best taken without direction or destination. Keeping to the open is best, and turning the eyes upward is recommended, especially on clear nights and most especially on the night of the new moon. On such nights, the heavens take on a special life. Only on the night of the new moon can one clearly see that the stars have different colors.

Overhead, a lonely jet streaked from north to south, so high that the sound of its engines did not reach me until its winking lights had nearly reached the horizon. I thought of the anonymous passengers, whose points of departure and arrival I would never know, and wondered if any had noticed the silent glow in the sky that their aircraft seemed to be fleeing.

Halfway across the field, I was stopped in my tracks by a sound that crossed the silent night. Five notes, uttered at instantly recognized intervals and shaped by a gutteral throat. Hoo-hoo, hoo, hoo, hoo. The sound has frightened countless inexperienced campers, and for many others become one of the most recognizable sounds of rural America. The call of a great horned owl.

Somewhere in the trees on the far side of the field, the two-foot bird perched and scanned the night with large, sensitive eyes. Quite suddenly my walk had gained purpose and direction.

The owl hooted again, louder but clearly from some distance away, possibly far beyond the boundaries of the field. Sound on a still night is deceptive. Distance and, at times, even direction cannot be estimated with certainty.

But I determined to follow as far as I could, step by sinking step through the crusted snow, the aurora forgotten, my eyes and ears turned in the direction of the sound. Step after step, I plunged through the snow, and, again and again, I heard the call that never grew closer. Hoo-hoo, hoo, hoo, hoo.

I reached the far side of the field and the edge of the trees. The most open forest, even under a full moon, seems an impenetrable jungle at night. What lay before me was far from open, an area of heavy underbrush and small swamps. Under the new moon, it was a place of dangerous shadows. For the first time, I became aware of the cold and the fact that I was nearly half a mile from home, with a tiring walk ahead of me.

The owl called again. Still distant; indeed, seemingly no closer than it had been when I first detected it. The bird waited in a tree somewhere ahead of me, but, if it waited for me, it would wait in vain. I turned my back to the trees and my eyes back to the aurora. I started back across the field.

Every minute or so as I walked, the great bird called out, the voice of a foghorn across a moonless sea of snow, the voice of wildness at my back, pursuing me as I trudged across the field. At last I reached the road, the sight of the lights of house, and the knowledge that a cup of cocoa was only a few minutes away. My legs trembled with the effort of slogging through the snow, and I was sweating, despite the chill. Cold had found my ears and face. The owl called again, the aurora shone on. It was nearly midnight on the night of the new moon. And all was well.

ℬ   ℭ

In the Heart of the Waterfall

Four inches of snow covered the ground. As I walked the narrow strip of land between a near-vertical cliff and a deep, flowing river, I found no trace of human visitors. The only tracks leading into the woods obviously had a four-legged origin. A wandering dog, I thought, perhaps a wolf. Whatever the creature's identity, it had long since come and gone. The tracks were half filled with wind-blown snow.

On a midwinter day when even sunlight felt cold, the clear sky meant quickly dropping temperatures come nightfall. But I was comfortable enough, as long as I kept moving.

Snow, ice, water, and dormant trees; a landscape of few colors and no life. I sensed no wind, nor any other movement. Occasional stirring of the river against a low-hanging branch or the splintering of shell ice from the river's edge was the only sound. No living creature showed itself, though I searched high and low. Even the birds favored silence.

I trudged through the near-pristine snow for almost an hour, struggling over large boulders cast down by the cliff, occasionally slipping where tiny springs, in freezing, had hidden sheets of ice beneath the snow. And then I came to the frozen waterfall.

One mile from the nearest road, a small creek followed the base of the cliff, eventually falling into a ravine joining the river. The fall was about eight feet. In spring, a raging torrent of water tumbled over the edge. In summer and autumn, the waterfall produced only a trickle. But winter, the season that captures and preserves every drop in ice, increased the waterfall beyond the imaginings of the stream that formed it.

A curtain of crystal higher than my head and perhaps one hundred feet wide lay before me. Before it stretched a field

of smooth snow—the frozen pool into which the stream fell. The surface of the ice appeared strong, a possible vantage point for photography. But I dared not test it. Ice with flowing water beneath it is often thin, and the pool below a waterfall often deep.

I circled to the top of the frozen cascade and looked down into the ravine. A shadowed opening in the curtain of ice seemed worthy of further investigation.

Above the falls, a thin shell of ice covered the creek. Little water lay beneath it. By carefully placing each footstep on one of the stones projecting through the ice, I was able to cross the frozen creek and climb down into the ravine on the other side.

The opening in the waterfall was rimmed by frozen spears that gave it an uncomfortable resemblance to a gaping mouth. Yet it was irresistibly inviting. On all fours, I crept onto the floor of the slick ice and into a wonderland.

In freezing, the waterfall had become a wall of translucent white, now lit by the afternoon sun to almost blinding intensity. A frost-rimed rock face formed the other wall of the cave I had entered, a twisting passage extending the full length of the fall. Fountains of ice emerged from the stone, showing

where simple trickles of water, aided by the cold, had created sculpture.

An elaborately shaped mass of ice about halfway across the waterfall blocked sight of anything beyond. I wanted to approach it, but dared not go more than a few feet into the cave. At some point, the slick ice floor supporting me would extend beyond the shoreline, and the dual threat of thin ice and deep water could not be ignored.

I sat on the ice, looking into the depths of the passage. It seemed infinitely colder inside the ice cave than it had been outside, impossibly lifeless and still. Not only did nothing move, but nothing visible seemed capable of movement.

But, as I listened, I heard it. Faintly at first but becoming obvious as I focused my ears and tried to ignore the chill penetrating my clothing. A whispering, only an echo of what had been and would be, but undeniably the sound of falling water. Behind tons of ice, locked within absolute stillness, the waterfall still flowed.

In the dead of winter, there is still life.

℘   ℧

Sticks and Stones

The beach was a narrow strip of stones, ranging in size from that of a pea to the size of my fist. Behind the beach stood an imposing bluff of sheer, fractured rock, and before it lay the cold, restless waters of Lake Superior. The only sound and movement came from the wind and the steady beat of waves against the shore. Occasionally one of the countless stones on the beach shifted slightly beneath the touch of the surf or as the soil beneath it settled.

It was a young beach, relatively speaking. The rounded stones littering it had only been there for an eyeblink or a million years, depending on whether one spoke in geological or human terms. Another eyeblink would find the stones reduced to sand. Water is a patient but relentless artisan. Day by day, a little more of the beach's stones was being washed away.

I found several bits of brick and concrete along the shore, each rounded by the water until it could be identified only after careful examination. Softer than stone, they had lost in a few decades what their counterparts had retained for millenia. Another generation would see the brick and cement worn away to nothing.

Here and there a leaf or twig was also cast up by the lake. A few days or weeks at best would find them gone, dissolved by water or rotted by the sun.

I thought it strange that the living, or at least the once-living, should lack the durability of the nonliving. Then I thought again.

Everything that exists holds a memory of some sort. The bits of brick whose relative perishability mocked man's efforts to imitate stone were memories of a building. They might have interesting tales to tell, could they speak.

114

The stones littering the beach remembered, too. Each held a memory of the cliffs behind the beach on which they rested, the sheer rock faces from which they had undoubtedly broken away. Those memories grow more remote each day. When the stones have been worn into dust by the action of the wind and water, they will be lost forever.

It is not so for the leaves and the bits of wood. They are the remains of life, and life does not forget.

In every leaf is the memory of the forest it had been, one leaf at a time, for as long as there have been leaves. Dropped by countless trees, rotted by countless wet springs and mingled with the dust of worn-away stones, every leaf finds its way back into the roots that supported it, or perhaps another set entirely. The nutrients that were the leaf and the stone become a leaf again. The cycle will continue as long as there are leaves and stones.

Living things wear out and are renewed again. Non-living things wear out and become living things. The ultimate progress of time is toward life.

No one knows why one collection of chemicals becomes a stone and another a leaf. The difference is life, universally admired and a continual source of wonder to us, even when we don't completely understand it. We do know that this intangible has been present, perhaps uniquely, on the earth for billions of years. With every opening of a flower, with every spreading of a leaf, we have another reminder that life will be around for a long time to come.

On the beach before me lay a grey stone smoothed and flattened by centuries of being rubbed against others by the water. I hefted it, aimed, and skimmed it across the surface of the lake. It delivered half a dozen satisfying skips before vanishing. Someday the lake will push it onto the beach again. It will be imperceptibly smaller, and somewhere in its shape, engraved too faintly for any eye in a language no living creature can read, will be the memory of the day I threw it into the water. With that memory will be countless others, also unreadable.

But the stone will be back. Everything comes back, given time. Robins return to the north each spring. Salmon, on reaching maturity, make their way to the very stream in which they were hatched or die trying. Even a forest burned to bare earth heals itself in a century or so, left to its own devices.

The leaves and the sticks littering the beach will be back someday. And I knew, as I turned away, that I would return as well.

℘   ℂ

Afterword

Spring follows winter, summer follows spring. Autumn lays summer to rest, and, at its end, winter comes again. In the natural world, change is the norm, and nature accepts it, knowing that what has been will soon return.

Since the writing of the essays in this book, road construction put an end to one of the ancient oaks. Excavation and transportation of gravel for the same project led first to temporary improvement, then removal of the last remnant of the Old Government Road. The northern night sky in my area is now washed by searchlights from a casino, making observation of the aurora borealis and most meteor showers impossible. Attempts to relocate the precise locations and objects inspiring several of the pieces have proven fruitless. The time for some things has passed, it seems, and the accidents that brought me others cannot be repeated on purpose. It is a rule by which much of nature seems to be governed.

Things change. We change. Children grow and move on with their lives. Ancestors die. Love affairs commenced with the promise of forever end in separation or divorce; others, commenced against all hope, bloom and endure. Through it all, the sun rises and sets, leaves swell in bud, then fall in dried glory when no longer needed, squirrels gather countless acorns and eat only a few, leaving the rest to sprout into oaks. In the deep ditch where the white oak defied the elements until the highway department made other plans, last spring saw a scattering of tiny three-leafed saplings. One or more, perhaps, will survive to maturity, though none now living will see them reach the size of their parent.

We are adrift on a mass of stone gigantic by our scale but barely a grain of sand on the shore of the cosmos. We circle a

single star in a sky filled with countless others. If there is anything of significance in our situation, it may be that we, perhaps uniquely, know who and where we are. Like all things, we
come and go, but unlike any other species, we leave deliberate
records of ourselves. On a rock face near the frozen waterfall, I
have found initials and dates carved by visitors more than a
century ago. Similar traces were left by the slaves who erected
the pyramids and the original settlers of Pompeii. We are the
only creatures to leave behind more than our bones. Whether
our hearts, minds, and hands are capable of leaving great
works of art or mere initials, we leave something more. And,
thereby, we keep alive the hope that we are something more. It
is that hope that turns the seasons of the heart.

I thank the reader for following in the footsteps of a few
of my wanderings. May your own be at least as fruitful. And
may you find, as I wish for all my friends—

Clear skies,
David Moffatt

        ℘   ଔ